Paving the Pathway
for Educational Success

Paving the Pathway for Educational Success

Effective Classroom Strategies for Students with Learning Disabilities

Nicholas D. Young,
Kristen Bonanno-Sotiropoulos,
and Teresa A. Citro

ROWMAN & LITTLEFIELD
Lanham • Boulder • New York • London

Published by Rowman & Littlefield
A wholly owned subsidiary of The Rowman & Littlefield Publishing Group, Inc.
4501 Forbes Boulevard, Suite 200, Lanham, Maryland 20706
www.rowman.com

Unit A, Whitacre Mews, 26-34 Stannary Street, London SE11 4AB

Copyright © 2018 by Nicholas D. Young, Kristen Bonanno-Sotiropoulos, and Teresa A. Citro

All rights reserved. No part of this book may be reproduced in any form or by any electronic or mechanical means, including information storage and retrieval systems, without written permission from the publisher, except by a reviewer who may quote passages in a review.

British Library Cataloguing in Publication Information Available

Library of Congress Cataloging-in-Publication Data

Names: Young, Nicholas D., 1967- author. | Bonanno-Sotiropoulos, Kristen, author. | Citro, Teresa Allissa, author.
Title: Paving the pathway for educational success : effective classroom strategies for students with learning disabilities / Nicholas D. Young, Kristen Bonanno-Sotiropoulos, and Teresa Allissa Citro.
Description: Lanham : Rowman & Littlefield, [2018] | Includes bibliographical references.
Identifiers: LCCN 2018000473 (print) | LCCN 2018001049 (ebook) | ISBN 9781475838862 (electronic) | ISBN 9781475838848 (cloth : alk. paper) | ISBN 9781475838855 (pbk. : alk. paper)
Subjects: LCSH: Learning disabilities—United States. | Learning disabled children—Education—United States. | Classroom environment—United States.
Classification: LCC LC4705 (ebook) | LCC LC4705 .Y68 2018 (print) | DDC 371.9—dc23
LC record available at https://lccn.loc.gov/2018000473

♾ ™ The paper used in this publication meets the minimum requirements of American National Standard for Information Sciences Permanence of Paper for Printed Library Materials, ANSI/NISO Z39.48-1992.

Printed in the United States of America

Contents

Preface		vii
Acknowledgments		xi
1	Fueling Success: Creating Caring Classrooms *Jacqueline Hawkins, Kristi L. Santi, and Erin Kolpek*	1
2	Learning, Behavioral, and Social Difficulties within a Multi-Tiered System of Supports: A Dynamic Perspective of Intervention Intensification *Kevin S. Sutherland, Thomas W. Farmer, Rachel L. Kunemund, and Brittany I. Sterrett*	15
3	Evidence-based Instructional Practices and Models to Assist Students with Learning Disabilities *Nicholas D. Young and Kristen Bonanno-Sotiropoulos*	33
4	Memory-Enhancing Strategies for Students with Learning Disabilities: Lessons Learned from Thirty-Five Years of Experimental Research *Margo A. Mastropieri, Thomas E. Scruggs, Anya Evmenova, and Kelley Regan*	45
5	Mnemonic Strategies: What Are They, How Can I Use Them, and How Effective Are They? *Margo A. Mastropieri, Thomas E. Scruggs, Kelley Regan, Anya Evmenova, and Judith Fontana*	63
6	Student Learning Profiles: Teaching with Style in Mind *Lynne M. Celli and Nicholas D. Young*	77

7 Instructional Strategies to Support the Writing Process for
   Students with Learning Disabilities as Well as Struggling Writers   87
   Nicholas D. Young and Kristen Bonanno-Sotiropoulos

8 Effective Home–School Partnerships: Strategies for Ensuring
   Collaboration for Families with Children with Learning Disabilities   97
   Nicholas D. Young and Elizabeth Jean

9 Effective Behaviors Employed by Successful Teachers of
   Students with Learning and Emotional Challenges: A
   Framework for Better Teaching   109
   Vance L. Austin

10 Ready to Learn: Helping Students Develop Positive Learning
    Outcomes through Effective Classroom Management   123
    Nicholas D. Young and Melissa A. Mumby

About the Primary Authors   133

Preface

Implementing successful classroom interventions is critical to promoting academic, social, and emotional success in all students but especially those with learning disabilities. To promote high-quality interventions for students, educators must arm themselves with the tools and knowledge necessary to identify and execute these practices. *Paving the Pathway for Educational Success: Effective Classroom Strategies for Students with Learning Disabilities* considers the unique characteristics that students with learning disabilities may display, the identification and use of evidence-based interventions, and the importance of teacher knowledge in supporting the teaching and learning process.

This book is designed to be a valuable resource for all educators who seek to gain a better understanding of learning disabilities, effective classroom practices, and meeting the instructional, emotional, and social needs of students with learning disabilities. Educators will benefit from the extensive research provided in the book and they will gain a thorough understanding of the importance of creating, supporting, and maintaining valuable interventions and how to do so effectively. The motivation for writing this book comes from several concerns:

- Our belief that creating safe learning environments, incorporating evidence-based intervention, is essential for students with learning disabilities;
- Our knowledge that approximately 42 percent of children receiving special education services are identified as having a learning disability (National Center for Learning Disabilities, 2014);
- Our awareness that students with learning disabilities can reach proficiency through consistent and effective teaching strategies;

- Our commitment to ensuring that all students experience positive academic, emotional, behavioral, and social gains;
- Our belief that efforts to encourage positive academic and social growth for all students must extend beyond the classroom door and incorporate collaborative efforts with families, peers, and other educators.

Chapter 1 presents a rationale for looking at education as the fuel for future success in life. The chapter explores what it means to develop twenty-first-century learners. Creating learning environments around a sense of belonging, building autonomy in learners, and creating caring and therapeutic classrooms and schools encourages student growth. For students with learning disabilities, positive classroom experiences can encourage them to view themselves as belonging, as successful, and as contributors to bright futures and careers.

Looking specifically at the academic, behavioral, and social difficulties of students with learning disabilities, chapter 2 discusses how problems in one of these three domains of functioning may influence students' adjustment in the other domains and how to consider appropriate intervention efforts. An overview of Response to Intervention (RTI) and Multi-Tiered System of Supports (MTSS) are discussed as well as the implications of a dynamic systems perspective for intervention efforts within specific tiers of support.

Chapter 3 addresses the concept of evidence-based interventions and models for students with learning disabilities. The characteristics of learning disabilities and how they affect the learning process are discussed. The authors explain the criteria standards for categorizing interventions as evidence based. Finally, the chapter looks at specific evidence-based strategies that can be used across all content areas.

As the book sought to balance research and practice, we are especially pleased to share chapters 4 and 5, which represent the best of this in a two-part sequence. Chapter 4 examines the research surrounding problems with semantic memory as the most commonly reported characteristics of learning disabilities. The authors discuss the benefits of the use of memory-enhancing strategies alone and in conjunction with other evidence-based strategies. Mnemonic strategies have proved to be powerful facilitators of academic learning and memory, resulting in effect sizes that are among the highest in all intervention research with students with learning disabilities.

Building on data in chapter 4, chapter 5 then takes the perspective of the practitioner and looks specifically at mnemonic (memory-enhancing) strategy instruction. Mnemonic strategies help make unfamiliar information more concrete and familiar by linking new information with prior knowledge using visual and auditory cues. The most effective mnemonic strategies use systematic encoding techniques and direct retrieval links to recently learned information.

A learning profile/learning style is often referred to as one's strong preference for taking in, processing, and mastering new information and new knowledge (McCarthy, 2014.). Chapter 6 examines the intersection of learning profiles, learning styles, and the research about learning disabilities. Focusing on individual learning styles, if made a major goal of every school and classroom and implemented appropriately, will ensure student success.

Chapter 7 looks specifically at evidence-based writing strategies. The Common Core State Standards places a large emphasis on written expression. This, in combination with high academic expectations, puts additional pressure on teachers to produce positive results. Students with learning disabilities experience high levels of frustration when it comes to the writing process. This chapter provides examples of evidence-based writing strategies that teachers can implement within their classrooms.

Stressing the importance of home–school partnerships, chapter 8 examines the connections that improve student outcomes. Positive home–school partnerships have been shown to play a critical role in a student's academic career. Bridging the two sides, home–school partnerships offer families a way to connect with their child and the environment in which he learns daily, while the educator has the chance to understand where the child comes from and who is important to them. This two-way communication is the basis for a long, healthy relationship; however, this process sometimes needs to be coaxed or is nonexistent.

Chapter 9 examines the behaviors of teachers who are effective at teaching students with disabilities. The author explores the research on successful inclusive teaching strategies, skills, and characteristics of proficient teachers. Ideas such as teacher attitudes, values, collaboration, and continuous learning are discussed.

Developing effective classroom management strategies is the focus of chapter 10. Classroom management is the first step in creating safe learning environments where learning can prosper. This chapter provides examples for developing and maintaining environments that are inclusive to a diverse population of students.

REFERENCES

McCarthy, J. (2014). How learning profiles can strengthen your teaching. *Edutopia*. Retrieved from https://www.edutopia.org/blog/learning-profiles-john-mccarthy.

National Center on Learning Disabilities. (2014). *The state of learning disabilities*. Retrieved from http://www.ncld.org/the-state-of-learning-disabilities-understanding-the-1-in-5.

Acknowledgments

We are indebted to Sue Clark for her keen eye and soft touch when carefully reviewing this manuscript. We will be forever grateful for her continued assistance.

Chapter One

Fueling Success

Creating Caring Classrooms

Jacqueline Hawkins, Kristi L. Santi, and Erin Kolpek, *University of Houston*

This chapter presents an overall rationale for viewing education as the fuel for future success in life, as energizing rather than energy zapping for both teachers and students—an educational process oftentimes in need of a remix as schools transform in the twenty-first century. Having set the stage for change in classrooms and schools, the chapter then focuses on three main aspects of research that will encourage all students, especially those with learning disabilities, to thrive in school.

Advancing a sense of belonging in students requires a keen focus on growth mind-set by all stakeholders, building autonomy in learners that lays the foundation for future self-regulation and success, and creating caring and therapeutic classrooms and schools that encourage student growth. Together these techniques can create opportunities for engagement in learner-centered activities, a greater degree of self-worth in students, and lifelong success for graduates. Students with learning disabilities can experience classrooms that encourage them to view themselves as belonging, as successful, and as contributors to bright futures and careers.

SETTING THE STAGE

Nationally, roughly 5 percent of students in schools have been formally identified as having a learning disability and about an additional 15 percent of students struggle in school with unidentified learning or attentional issues (Cortiella and Horowitz, 2014). That's one in every five students or four to five students in a typical classroom. The National Center for Learning Disabilities (2014) relates that two-thirds of students with learning disabilities are male, disproportionate numbers live in poverty, students are more likely to be in foster care, and many are English-language learners or minority students.

Students with learning disabilities experience lower grades and higher course failure; lower passing rates on standardized assessments are common. Half of students with learning disabilities also have a record of disciplinary action, and only about two out of every three students graduate with a regular diploma. Clearly, for many students identified with learning disabilities, there is more going on in their lives than challenges with academic content.

Seminal research confirms what many teachers have known: there are consistent similarities in the performance of students in academic and social contexts irrespective of whether they have been formally identified as having a learning disability (Francis, Shaywitz, Stuebing, Shaywitz, and Fletcher, 1996). More than forty years after the passage of the Education for All Handicapped Children Act in 1975, it's clear that focusing on the success of students with disabilities, and their unidentified peers who also struggle, is a positive option for educators.

FUELING SUCCESS

Energizing students for future life and work success may feel like a lofty goal. Educators are often daunted by the enormity of the task of supporting students through successful completion of the academic year and contributing to their progress to graduation. Each student's life after graduation day is perhaps considered to be beyond an educator's control; however, actions that educators take during each student's time in school can have a positive and long-lasting impact on the future. When we consider that education is the fuel to a future economic engine, it situates the importance of an educator's role in a different light.

The economic success of the community, the state, and the nation is changed by the success of its citizens. Education fuels that future success, and the economy needs all individuals to maximize the contribution they can make to fuel that success. Students with learning disabilities are able to contribute to that bright future, and caring classrooms and schools can encourage them to do just that.

Connecting future economic progress into daily activities in classrooms can be hard. Educators may need to focus outside the boundaries of schools and classrooms to help build the connections. Understanding what employers need will help illustrate what can occur today and how relevant student content knowledge, social skills, and an ability to self-regulate behavior will be to that future success.

The State of Texas Workforce Commission, for example, asked employers to describe the skill sets needed for workers across six broad industry clusters. Results show that workers need content knowledge that's unique to their chosen profession, should have the skills to work in teams and with colleagues, and should possess essential skills like time-management, organization, and follow-through (Texas Workforce Commission, 2016).

These outcomes should be familiar for educators since they relate to academic success in the content areas, social success in behavior and attendance, and self-regulatory and self-efficacy skills that build personal success and a sense of belonging. Essentially, the skills that future employers report for job-related success are the very skills that educators foster in classrooms and schools across the nation. They are the very skills that are documented goals on countless Individualized Education Plans (IEPs).

ENERGIZED FOR LIFE

Many students, and indeed some of their teachers, find school to be humdrum. In the day-to-day activities in which teachers and students engage in classrooms, the long-term goals of schools are often forgotten. As we focus on assignments, timelines, tests, and "checking things off our list," the lives of students and teachers frequently get lost in the shuffle. That can be especially true for students who struggle academically and socially. Students who have been identified as having a learning disability often feel that the focus is on the very things that can challenge them the most: reading, writing, mathematics, and getting things done.

The everyday emphasis is on the grade, the deadline, and the score on a standardized test rather than why they engage in those activities or their relevance to the future. Although doing well on assignments, working to a deadline, and passing a test are all aspects that can contribute to their future, the ultimate goal of schools is to prepare lifelong learners who are energized by both their life and their work as they transition through adulthood: energized to keep learning, energized to remain motivated, energized to engage with others.

To develop and harness this energy, classrooms must be caring environments where all students experience success, where all students gain a sense of belonging, and where all students develop autonomy. Caring and therapeutic structures and practices can be engineered by educators to ensure success for all students. That success also can become reciprocal. Specifically, the success of the students energizes educators to try different options, look for different supports, see classrooms in a different light, and encourage students to take the lead in their own learning.

Within these caring structures, success fuels success and educators who engage with students feel spurred on to provide greater opportunities. Assignments, timelines, and tests continue to exist; however, they are approached with a different mind-set, they are evaluated from different perspectives, and they are managed by learners rather than educators. Classrooms become safer places to be and learners can become energized for life. However, given concerns about graduation rates, an educated workforce, and the increasing demand for an ever more tech-savvy workforce, it's apparent that the "mix" for education's fuel needs some adjustment if education's engine is to purr along.

TIME FOR A REMIX

Nationally, nearly 95 percent students with disabilities are educated in the general education setting for some portion of the school day (US Department of Education, 2016) with the majority (62.6 percent) in general education classrooms for more than 80 percent of the school day, an increase of 10 percent in the last decade. Although this is encouraging, it also underlines the increasing responsibility of general educators for the education of students with disabilities and for leaders who know how to support general education, inclusive environments, and systems change to support a variety of teaching arrangements.

General education teachers report that they lack the necessary skills and knowledge to effectively provide instruction to students with disabilities and often approach students with disabilities from a deficit model lens (Schiller, Bobronnikov, O'Reilly, Price, and St. Pierre, 2005; Lalvani, 2013). Quashing the deficit model approach needs to begin with a learner-centered approach that focuses on the strengths of individual students. If we take a learner-centered perspective and look at what students need from school, rather than what school needs from students, we may have a way forward.

As humans, we've spent millennia searching for a sense of belonging. We've come together in family groups, small communities, and larger tribes to build a sense of safety, a sense of autonomy, and a sense of personal value to others. However, often a sense of belonging, value, and caring is not experienced by students with learning disabilities. Research demonstrates that educators need help to develop a different type of classroom that supports the needs of students with learning disabilities. Essentially, the need to adjust from a deficit model to a growth model that encourages all students to perform well and contribute to society is necessary.

What is needed is a remix of evidence-based facets. These involve the promotion and development of growth mind-sets by all stakeholders, the focus on self-regulation for learners, and the generation of therapeutic structures where students are nurtured and supported by caring educators in caring classrooms.

Remix #1 Growth Mind-set

Embrace the growth mind-set that all individuals matter and can make a positive contribution. By doing so, we can make collective progress, we become more learner centered, and we build a sense of belonging for our students and families. Fixed and growth mind-sets are two implicit theories of intelligence that many people consider to influence psychological and performance-oriented aspects of life that include efforts when work becomes difficult; the role of effort, help-seeking, and trying different strategies in becoming "smart"; and, finally, the impact that mind-set shifts can have on performance (Yeager and Walton, 2011).

A fixed mind-set espouses that intelligence and talent were fixed at birth and do not change (Dweck, 2006). Students with a fixed mind-set tend to give less effort when work gets hard or try to avoid hard work altogether. They demonstrate negative effort beliefs that are unproductive, are less resilient to obstacles in their way, don't always respond positively to challenges (Blackwell, Trzesniewski, and Dweck, 2007; Yeager and Dweck, 2012), and often underperform academically.

Alternatively, students with a growth mind-set believe that talent and intelligence can be learned and that they can make incremental improvements over time. Students can grow their brains with hard work and effort, by asking for help, and by engaging in new learning strategies (Dweck, 2015). Students with growth mind-sets tend to meet or exceed the challenges, are more motivated, and will produce work to a higher standard. According to Dweck (2006), "People in a growth mindset don't just seek challenge, they thrive on it. The bigger the challenge, the more they stretch" (p. 21).

Students with growth mind-sets tend to seek more difficult tasks and demonstrate greater resilience when facing obstacles or failure. Building a sense of belonging for students through mind-set changes must occur at all levels to include: community, parent, teacher, and student mind-sets. As educators and communities review mind-set research and its potential impact on student outcomes, they should consider aligning mind-sets and expectations at these various levels to build a sense of belonging for every student and every family.

Community Mind-set Action Steps

Community growth mind-set focuses the expectation on the whole school: every student—irrespective of actual or perceived capacity—is successful, valued, and belongs.

- Review school mission statement. Revise, if necessary, to focus on all students' success.
- Develop community pledges that value the contributions of all individuals.
- Build a sense of belonging through changes in community mind-set.

Parent Mind-set Action Steps

Parent mind-set can differ depending on family circumstances, prior experiences, and perceptions of their children. For example, parents of students with disabilities may discuss the different perceptions that others have about their children, their experiences with inclusive classrooms or classrooms that do not provide the level of support that their child needs to succeed. In some cultures, disabilities are seen as a gift while in others they are seen as a deficit. Helping to engage parents in a growth mind-set with their children is important. Parents can learn how educators will discuss their children, how to set reasonable expectations, encourage their performance and recognize the achievements of their children.

- Use person-first language to describe students at all times. This means that the person or individual is spoken about first. For example, consistent use of the term *student with a learning disability* is person-first language. Person-first language dignifies the human being rather than highlighting a disability.
- Discuss reasonable expectations for children with their parents. Many of us can say that we want the best for our children but understanding the implications of that is often difficult to articulate. Like the children's story "Goldilocks and the Three Bears," we have to get things "just right" for students. If we set expectations that are too high or too low, success may not be the outcome. Too-high expectations may result in failure and an unwillingness to try in the future; too-low expectations may result in inadvertent insults and boredom that exacerbates students' perceptions of their challenges. "Just right" expectations can promote manageable progress and ultimate success.
- Encourage children to stretch their performance. Students who feel a little challenge are usually up for that challenge—especially if educators and parents have set reasonable expectations and are there to encourage their efforts. Encouraging students to do more, work more accurately, and beat

their own time can help them stretch their performance while enjoying the challenge.
- Comment on and encourage effort. Often, students with disabilities may not get things correct on the first attempt (indeed, most of us don't) and need encouragement to work through the challenge and give a good effort. Effort, when sustained, is a good indication of future success. External recognition of that effort, by a parent or educator, goes far to changing the mind-set of a child.

Teacher Mind-set Action Steps

Teacher mind-set often focuses on the variety of students in a classroom and the breadth of lessons and activities they must prepare to ensure success. Some educators focus their efforts on the largest group of students, those who are generally in the middle of the pack academically, since their efforts can have an impact on a larger proportion of students. This can mean that students who struggle and students who excel can fail to benefit from instruction. Engaging in a learner-centered mind-set, implementing differentiated instruction, and focusing on progress monitoring can create substantial shifts in classroom engagement and each student's sense of belonging.

- Change from a teacher-centered mind-set to a learner-centered mind-set can be a very liberating step for teachers and a very constructive step for students in their class. A learner-centered mind-set focuses on individual students and their needs. It shifts an educator's mind-set from "What do I want to do?" to "What do students need to learn?"
- Differentiate instruction (Tomlinson, 2014) to meet the needs of individual students rather than the needs of the group as a whole. The provision of instruction and activities at different levels of difficulty can challenge and stretch students as they engage in their own performance.
- Focus on progress monitoring rather that normative assessment. This means that assessment becomes about each individual student's performance over time. Student performance at the beginning of the year is compared with that at midyear or the end of the year. Progress over time rather than a comparison with others who may have different capacities and needs helps to motivate individuals and appreciate their value.

Student Mind-set Action Steps

Student mind-set is a learned strategy where they are taught how to promote personal resilience. It teaches students how to adjust the mind-set they hold about their personal characteristics and how to become more resilient when facing challenges—both academic and social (Yeager and Dweck, 2012).

When student mind-sets shift to focus on what they can do to adjust outcomes, they become more willing to try different paths to success.

- Teach students to "grow their brains." This step helps students focus on the type of effort they are putting forth and whether it has been working. If the outcomes have not been as intended, students need to "grow their brain" by engaging in different strategies and accessing helping from others.
- Offer students strategies in which they can engage in various situations. Provide a variety of instructional and social strategies that have been demonstrated to be effective. Support students through the use of these strategies and provide time for discussion of outcomes.
- Engage learner-center assessment techniques that compare student performance over time. Students become their own model; self-comparison over time versus group comparison and ranking can help change mind-sets. Students can see their own growth and can determine the next steps they need to take to meet their goals.
- Provide self-regulation opportunities throughout academic and social time. Promote self-graphing of performance (Alberto and Troutman, 2016) as an essential component of self-regulated learning to help students to visualize their progress over time and help them to develop a growth mind-set.

Remix #2 Self-Regulation

Here it is important to build a sense of autonomy that lays the foundation for future self-regulation and success for students as they become increasingly more independent and more able to say "Yes, I can!" In a seminal study called Schools without Failure (Glasser, 1969), students were provided with safe opportunities to try new things. Sometimes the students were successful and other times they were not.

The focus of Schools without Failure (1969) was trying and learning from each of those attempts. Increasing student responsibility for their actions, improving communication and social interactions with peers and teachers, and helping students to see the value of education were the goals of Schools without Failure. The classroom format and the process of helping to create an environment in which students succeed academically and are encouraged to take responsibility for their own learning promotes success.

Students were encouraged to discuss their own lives, their current circumstances, and how they thought the future would unfold. Self-diagnostic discussions revolved around academic topics and social interactions in which they had been involved and what the outcomes were. When challenges occurred, discussions would ensue several times per week to permit students to have some control over the classroom environment. Teacher behaviors changed over time and students believed more strongly in the importance of school (Masters and Laverty, 1977).

Schools without Failure provides an important backdrop to the implementation of caring classrooms. Students in caring classrooms need to be heard and the discussion format of Schools without Failure supports that type of direct engagement in the learning process. Schools without Failure can be used as a precursor to the implementation of a self-regulated learning approach that develops skills in students with learning disabilities that will serve them well in their future college and career.

Self-regulated learning (SRL) has been prevalent since Bandura introduced the concept in 1971 and remains relevant today as a model that focuses students' motivation, engagement, and academic achievement (Wolters and Hoops, 2015). SRL is a foundation for lifelong learning, and students who engage in SRL more frequently tend to be more successful learners (Merriam and Bierema, 2014; Bail, Zhang, and Tachiyama, 2008).

Bandura (1986) further outlined self-regulation as opportunities for students to pay attention to what they are doing (self-observation), determine whether what they have done is successful (self-evaluation), and make adjustments to their academic or social behavior based on their determination of success (self-reaction). Learners can engage in behaviors that help them manage their learning time (e.g., use of a planner to develop their schedule or an alarm clock to get to class on time), control their environment (e.g., light, temperature, seating arrangement), or track their performance over time (e.g., self-graphing).

Irrespective of the context, students who have developed self-regulated learning skills can set goals; monitor their own work during learning; compare their performance over time and to a target; and connect the dots between their learning, motivation, and behavior with the outcomes they achieve. They can ask themselves, "In the future, do I keep doing the same or do I engage different strategies or help from someone else?"

Self-regulated Learning Action Step

- Before: Engage students in creating their own goals (both for their future and class expectations) and strategies that they will engage with to meet their goals.
- During: Teach students to monitor their own learning, motivations, and behavior as they perform the tasks.
- After: Teach students to compare their current performance with their prior performance to date (e.g., personal progress), the criterion for the class (e.g., standard for passing), or a national measure (e.g., national ranking) to help them determine the extent to which they are meeting or

exceeding their goals. This also helps students reflect on how the strategies in which they engage may need to be adjusted so they can meet their goal in the future.
- Rinse and Repeat: Demonstrate how the link between self-regulation and knowing the outcome of their efforts can spur them on to improve their performance over time.

Although these action steps appear to be linear, educators find themselves moving backward and forward between the steps as they work with students to ensure they become self-regulated learners. This recursive process ensures that educators are using student progress to create the caring classrooms that are necessary for success.

Remix #3 Caring Classroom

Creating caring and therapeutic classrooms and schools encourages students to meet challenges in a safe environment and realize their future potential. Abrams (2005) provided an overview of how therapeutic teachers can promote the academic success of all learners. Although his work supports the needs of teachers who work with students who engage in challenging behaviors, the recommendations made apply to teachers and classrooms for *all* learners.

Therapeutic teachers create environments in which students can thrive both academically and socially. Successful therapeutic classrooms hinge on teachers who take care of their own health and that of their students, who treat their students with dignity and get to know and understand their needs, and who set realistic expectations and deliver exemplary instruction that promotes student success.

Self-care and student care are the underpinnings of therapeutic classrooms. Self-care for educators is essential to their ability to focus on supporting students. Therapeutic teachers engage in stress-management techniques that help them manage their mental health. Only when they are healthy can they have the energy and drive to support their students. Therapeutic teachers have a healthy attitude to both their job and their students and have learned to listen carefully, be circumspect in what they say, and be respectful and confident in how they approach their job (Abrams, 2005; Kaufman, 2001).

Bonding with students occurs when therapeutic teachers get to know their students well. Therapeutic teachers most likely have prior assessments, documents from student files, and comments from others, but their main focus is on talking with students and getting to know their needs, work habits, and preferences. Based on this information, they develop realistic plans with students that promote success and help students engage with their own individual plan—adjusting, as necessary. Therapeutic teachers must believe that the goals and plans that have been set are achievable since unrealistic expectations can set students (and teachers) up for failure.

Instilling confidence in students to succeed means that teachers must possess excellent instructional skills that provide students with the confidence that their teachers know what they are doing, possess strategies that students can engage with when necessary, and are an access point for help should the need arise. Further, teacher instructional skills will generate student confidence in their own ability to be successful. Everyone in the classroom, students and teachers alike, is improving their skills, communicating well, and managing the stress that's part of change and growth. Everyone believes that success is both possible and expected.

Therapeutic Classroom Action Steps

- Manage stress in the classroom by setting realistic goals, provide adequate support, and meet student needs.
- Listen to what students have to say, focus on their strengths, and encourage (teach) them to engage in self-regulation.
- Provide a variety of instructional strategies that can promote academic and/or social success.
- Be there for students and let them know you are there should help be sought. Teacher focus is on the success of students rather than distractions that can take everyone off the goal.
- Develop a classroom support structure that ensures there are options outside a classroom that can be engaged should the need arise.

FINAL THOUGHTS

Creating caring classrooms may feel like a daunting task; however, all components of each facet do not need to be ready to implement on Day 1. When educators take an inventory to assess the mind-set of their students, campus, and campus stakeholders, when they understand the basics of learner-centered principles, as well as the role that self-regulation can have in that process, and when they focus on therapeutic teaching to support students, they have the beginnings of a plan for moving forward.

Educators may choose to follow the basic Plan, Do, Study, Act (PDSA) process to help them to fine-tune their classroom as additional information is learned and different needs are identified. With time, they will have created an asset map for their classroom (and themselves), conducted a strengths analysis and needs assessment for each individual student, and fueled the success of all students in their care. Being in a constant state of remix is to be expected and relished as future generations of students are energized for life.

POINTS TO REMEMBER

- *Students with learning disabilities can experience classrooms that encourage them to view themselves as belonging, as successful, and as contributors to bright futures and careers when educators adjust classrooms.*
- *Employers report that the very skills that educators foster in classrooms and schools across the nation are the skills required for job-related success. These are the very skills that are documented goals on countless Individualized Education Plans for students with learning disabilities.*
- *Research demonstrates that educators need help to develop a different type of classroom that supports the needs of students with learning disabilities. Essentially, they need to adjust from a deficit model to a growth model that encourages all students to perform well and contribute to society.*
- *Educators can adjust classrooms and advance a sense of belonging in students by focusing on a growth mind-set by all stakeholders, building autonomy in learners that lays the foundation for future self-regulation and success, and creating caring and therapeutic classrooms and schools that encourage student growth. By doing so, we can make collective progress, we become more learner centered, and we build a sense of belonging for our students and families.*
- *Adjustments continue to be made over time, for different students, and in diverse contexts. The Plan, Do, Study, Act (PDSA) process helps fine-tune classrooms as additional information is learned and different needs are identified.*

The primary chapter author can be reached at jhawkins@uh.edu.

REFERENCES

Abrams, B. J. (2005). Becoming a therapeutic teacher for students with emotional and behavioral disorders. *Teaching Exceptional Children,* 38(2), 40–45. https://doi.org/10.1177/004005990503800205.

Alberto, P., and Troutman, A. (2016). *Applied behavior: Analysis for teachers.* 9th ed. North York, ON: Pearson Education.

Bail, F. T., Zhang, S., and Tachiyama, G. T. (2008). Effects of a self-regulated learning course on the academic performance and graduation rate of college students in an academic support program. *Journal of College Reading and Learning,* 39(1), 54–73. https://doi.org/10.1080/10790195.2008.10850312.

Bandura, A. (1986). *Social foundations of thought and action: A social cognitive theory.* Bergen County, NJ: Prentice-Hall.

Blackwell, L. A., Trzesniewski, K. H., and Dweck, C. S. (2007). *Implicit theories of intelligence predict achievement across an adolescent transition: A longitudinal study and an intervention.* Retrieved from https://www.ncbi.nlm.nih.gov/pubmed/17328703.

Cortiella, C., and Horowitz, S. H. (2014). *The state of learning disabilities: Facts, trends and emerging issues.* New York: National Center for Learning Disabilities.

Dweck, C. S. (2006). *Mindset*. New York, NY: Random House.

Dweck, C. S. (2015). Carol Dweck revisits the "Growth Mindset." *Education Week*, September 15. Retrieved from http://www.edweek.org/ew/articles/2015/09/23/carol-dweck-revisits-the-growthmindset.html.

Francis, D. J., Shaywitz, S. E., Stuebing, K. K., Shaywitz, B. A., and Fletcher, J. M. (1996). Developmental lag versus deficit models of reading disability: A longitudinal, individual growth curves analysis. *Journal of Educational Psychology*, 88, 3–17. Retrieved from https://eric.ed.gov/?id=EJ526854.

Glasser, W. (1969). *Schools without failure*. New York: Random House.

Kauffman, J. (2001). *Characteristics of emotional and behavioral disorders of children and youth*. 7th ed. Upper Saddle River, NJ: Merrill Prentice Hall.

Lalvani, P. (2013). Privilege, compromise, or social justice: Teachers' conceptualizations of inclusive education. *Disability and Society*, 28(1), 14–27. Retrieved from https://eric.ed.gov/?id=EJ990204.

Masters, J. R., and Laverty, G. E. (1977). The relationship between changes in attitude and changes in behavior in the schools without failure program. *Journal of Research and Development in Education*, 10, 36–49. Retrieved from https://eric.ed.gov/?id=EJ157987.

Merriam, S. B., and Bierema, L. L. (2014). *Adult learning: Bridging theory and practice*. San Francisco: Jossey-Bass.

National Center on Learning Disabilities. (2014). *The state of learning disabilities*. Retrieved from: http://www.ncld.org/the-state-of-learning-disabilities-understanding-the-1-in-5.

Schiller, E., Bobronnikov, E., O'Reilly, F., Price, C., and St. Pierre, R. (2005). *Placing and serving children with disabilities in the LRE. In the study of state and local implementation and impact of the Individuals with Disabilities Education Act: Final 2nd Interim Report (2002–2003 School Year)*. Bethesda, MD: ABT Associates.

Texas Workforce Commission. (2016). *Workplace essential skills [web report]*. Retrieved from http://www.lmci.state.tx.us/shared/PDFs/Workplace_Essential_Skills_Final.pdf.

Tomlinson, C. A. (2014). *The differentiated classroom: Responding to the needs of all learners*. 2nd ed. Alexandria, VA: Association for Supervision and Curriculum Development.

University of Kansas, School of Education. (2017). *Timeline of the Individuals with Disabilities Education Act*. Retrieved from https://educationonline.ku.edu/community/idea-timeline.

US Department of Education, Office of Special Education and Rehabilitative Services, Office of Special Education Programs (2016). *38th annual report to congress on the implementation of the Individuals with Disabilities Education Act, 2016*. Washington, DC. Retrieved from https://www2.ed.gov/about/reports/annual/osep/index.html.

Wolters, C. A., and Hoops, L. D. (2015). Self-regulated learning interventions for motivationally disengaged college students. In T. L. Cleary (ed.), *Self-regulated learning interventions with at-risk youth: Enhancing adaptability, performance, and well-being* (pp. 67–88). Washington, DC: American Psychological Association.

Yeager, D. S., and Dweck, C. S. (2012). Mindsets that promote resilience: When students believe that personal characteristics can be developed. *Educational Psychologist*, 47(4), 302–14. https://doi.org/10.1080/00461520.2012.722805.

Yeager, D. S., and Walton, G. M. (2011). Social-psychological interventions in education: They're not magic. *Review of Educational Research*, 81(2), 267–301. https://doi.org/10.3102/0034654311405999.

Chapter Two

Learning, Behavioral, and Social Difficulties within a Multi-Tiered System of Supports

A Dynamic Perspective of Intervention Intensification

Kevin S. Sutherland, *Virginia Commonwealth University*; Thomas W. Farmer, *College of William and Mary*; Rachel L. Kunemund, *Virginia Commonwealth University*; and Brittany I. Sterrett, *Virginia Commonwealth University*

The educational outcomes of students with learning disabilities (LD) reflect many influences. Family, biological, school, and community factors are but a few influences that may contribute to the developmental trajectory of all students. Typically, teachers have varying levels of impact on these factors. To illustrate, a teacher cannot change the family structure, but s/he can develop communication with the family, potentially encouraging increased involvement with the school now and into the future. At the same time, teachers tend to have considerable impact on the academic, behavioral, and social experiences of students and the potential interplay between these domains within the classroom and school context.

As schools work to establish Multi-Tiered System of Supports (MTSS) to bridge these three domains of student functioning, it is critical for teachers to not only understand how to enhance students' performance in each domain but also to know how these domains can support or constrain each other (Samuels, 2016).

The purposes of this chapter are threefold. First, we briefly discuss the academic, behavioral, and social difficulties of students with LD from a dynamic systems perspective. The goals of this section are to discuss how problems in one of these three domains of functioning may influence students' adjustment in the other domains and to consider how dynamic processes across domains may affect intervention efforts. Second, we provide a brief overview of MTSS and discuss the implications of a dynamic systems perspective for intervention efforts within specific tiers of support.

Third, we discuss the concept of intervention intensification and we consider the implications of a dynamic systems perspective for implementing tailored, data-driven strategies that are individualized to students' specific strengths and needs, with a specific focus on peer influences and teacher-student interactions. We end with a brief example describing how a teacher integrates her understanding of the dynamic systems of her classroom and a student's intensive behavioral needs to design an intensive intervention that has promise for impacting the student's academic, behavioral, and social development.

LEARNING DISABILITIES, DYNAMIC SYSTEMS, AND SCHOOL ADJUSTMENT PROBLEMS

Students with LD, by definition, do not achieve adequately in one or more key domains of learning (i.e., oral expression, listening comprehension, written expression, basic reading skills, reading fluency skills, reading comprehension, mathematics calculation, mathematics problem solving) for the child's age when provided with appropriate instruction and when the learning difficulty cannot be attributed to another disability (England, Butler, and Gonzalez, 2015). Yet there is considerable variability in the learning needs and associated difficulties of students who experience learning problems and/or are identified for special education services for LD.

It is possible, for example, to identify distinct profiles of students with LD who do or do not have comorbid math and reading disabilities (Fuchs, Fuchs, and Compton, 2012). Likewise, students with LD may have distinct social and behavioral profiles depending on other factors that may or may not be directly associated with the disability (Al-Yagon, 2016; Frederickson and Furnham, 2004; Vallance, Cummings, and Humphries, 1998). The importance of this distinction is that students with LD who are distinguished by different profiles of school functioning may respond differentially to specific interventions. Therefore, it is important to understand variability in the academic, behavioral, and social functioning of students with LD.

A dynamic systems perspective of human development (Kunnen, 2012) helps provide important insights into the learning difficulties, school adjustment problems, and differential intervention needs of students with LD who experience distinct profiles or patterns of school functioning. The dynamic systems perspective is central to developmental science and involves clarifying how multiple factors and processes contribute to human functioning and outcomes (Cairns, 2000; Sameroff, 2000; Smith and Thelen, 2003; Kunnen, 2012).

Three core features of a dynamic systems perspective are germane to the present discussion. First, multiple domains of functioning operate as an interconnected system that collectively contribute to the adaptation and trajectory of the development of the individual (Magnusson and Cairns, 1996; Sameroff, 2000). Second, the interactions among individuals and/or other factors within the school ecology are transactional, which means they have the continual potential to constrain or change each other (Bronfenbrenner, 1996; Cairns, 2000; Sameroff, 2009). Third, there are multiple pathways to the same outcomes for different children (equi-finality) and the same variables and pathways may lead to distinct outcomes for different youth (multi-finality) (Cairns and Cairns, 1994; Sameroff, 2000; Smith and Thelen, 2003).

Developmental science has important implications for special education both in terms of understanding students' school adaptation and for developing multifactored interventions aimed at enhancing the developmental pathways and outcomes of students with disabilities (Farmer, Gatzke-Kopp, Lee, Dawes, and Talbott, 2016). The three features of dynamic systems described provide important guidance for interventions to support the adaptation and adjustment of students with LD.

An Interconnected System of Multiple Domains of School Functioning

There are three distinct domains of functioning in school: academic, behavioral, and social. Although each of these domains can be viewed singularly, to understand their contributions to a student's long-term outcomes it is useful to think of them as being part of a system of correlated factors that collectively affect the student's overall school adjustment (Cairns and Cairns, 1994; Roeser and Peck, 2003).

In other words, students develop as an integrated whole and when we focus only on single variables we do so at the risk of overlooking the interplay between factors in development and adaptation (Bergman and Vargha, 2013; Magnusson and Cairns, 1996). The importance of this point is that multiple domains in a dynamic system tend to be linked bidirectionally and the functioning of one domain may support or constrain the functioning of other domains as well as specific outcomes of interest (Bronfenbrenner, 2005; Cairns, 2000; Gottlieb, 1996).

From a dynamic systems perspective, clarifying the nature of a student's learning problems and determining how to address these problems instructionally is only the beginning. It is also important to determine if the student is experiencing behavioral and/or social difficulties, how these difficulties relate to the student's disability, and whether and how they may affect intervention efforts.

Among students with LD, for example, it is possible to identify a range of school functioning profiles (Farmer, Rodkin, Pearl, and Van Acker, 1999; Farmer, Gatzke-Kopp, et al., 2016). Some students with LD may respond well to intervention and are represented by profiles that indicate good adjustment across the academic, behavioral, and social domains. Other students may have profiles that reflect a single difficulty (i.e., academic) but are doing well behaviorally and socially. Some students may have multirisk profiles that are characterized by difficulties both academically and in one of the other two domains (behaviorally, socially). A few students will have high-risk profiles distinguished by difficulties across all three domains.

As we develop interventions to provide support for students with LD, it is probably not realistic to expect students represented by these different profiles to have the same intervention needs or to respond to intervention in the same ways. When students experience a single risk, it is important to provide supports that prevent risks from developing in the other domains (Farmer and Farmer, 2001).

In contrast, when students experience multiple risks, it is important to consider how risks across domains contribute to each other and to the student's overall school adjustment. Multifactored interventions can be coordinated to reorganize this system of risks by providing supports that promote new skills and strengths (Farmer, 2013; Farmer, Sutherland, et al., 2016).

Transactions among Students and Their Environments

Students do not develop in a vacuum and their skills and abilities do not simply unfold or emerge over time as they grow older. Instead, development is a continuous and ongoing process that involves synchronized and adaptive interactions with one's ecology (Bronfenbrenner, 1996; Cairns, 2000). This process of synchronization and adaptation is transactional in the sense that there are interchanges in which both individuals and their environments take on new capacities and characteristics in response to each other (Cairns, 1979; Sameroff, 2009). This means direct, intentional interventions are not the only influences on students' academic performance, engagement, behavior, and adjustment.

The ecology itself, how students are engaged by it, and how the context responds to students can all shape, change, constrain, and/or reinforce students' behavior and adaptation. This is important both because aspects of the context can affect the impact of interventions and because contexts can be managed to support intervention activities (Farmer, Reinke, and Brooks, 2014). As we move forward with MTSS and intervention intensification, we must be careful to not only focus on evidence-based practices but also leverage the management of the ecology to support more directed interventions (Farmer, Sutherland, et al., 2016; Farmer et al., 2017).

Multiple Pathways and Outcomes

The concept that there are multiple pathways to the same outcomes for different children and also that the same variables and pathways may lead to distinct outcomes for different youth is critical as we utilize MTSS to deliver services based on how students respond to intervention. A central concept of MTSS is that there are standardized practices that are generally effective for all children and when students are not responsive to standard, research-proven, evidence-based practices, they likely need more intensive forms of intervention (Cook and Odom, 2013; Danielson and Rosenquist, 2014; Ludlow, 2014).

MTSS focuses on supports that address the academic, behavioral, and social domains of school functioning (Lane, Carter, Jenkins, Dwiggins, and Germer, 2015). Standardized interventions and a tiered system to guide efforts to match intervention strategies to students' level of responsiveness are important advancements in the delivery of special education services. Yet there is a need to have a service delivery framework that is not solely yoked to standardized interventions but also takes into consideration data about individual learners within the specific instructional or classroom context (Farmer, Sutherland, et al., 2016; Fuchs and Fuchs, 2015).

Two distinct, but related, forms of data are important here. First, within the umbrella term of LD it is possible to identify subtypes of learners that reflect distinct profiles of academic, behavioral, and social data (Al-Yagon, 2016; Farmer, Rodkin, et al., 1999; Fuchs et al., 2012). Second, students within specific profiles of adjustment may be affected by how they experience the context including their peer group affiliations and experiences, their relationships with teachers, and the composition and social structure of the classroom (Ahn and Rodkin, 2014; Farmer et al., 2017; Hendrickx, Mainhard, Boor-Klip, Cillessen, and Brekelmans, 2016).

From this perspective, we contend that it is important to understand that intervention efforts may be strengthened by going beyond whether a student has a LD and whether the student is responsive to a specific intervention. The developmental concepts of equi- and multi-finality suggest that students' adaptation and outcomes in relation to specific strategies can be nuanced depending on their own characteristics and the characteristics of the ecology (Farmer, Gatzke-Kopp, et al., 2016).

As MTSS and intervention intensification move forward, there is a need to identify how distinct profiles of adjustment and contextual factors operate in relation to specific intervention strategies in an effort to further refine and tailor interventions to students' specific developmental characteristics and the contexts they experience.

A DYNAMIC PERSPECTIVE OF MULTI-TIERED SYSTEM OF SUPPORTS

Multi-Tiered System of Supports (MTSS) is a systematic approach for providing evidence-based practices to address students' academic, behavioral, and social needs within a tiered framework of increasingly intensive levels of support (Samuels, 2016; Lane et al., 2015). Tier 1 involves universal strategies designed to support all students and provide a foundation for more specialized intervention.

Tier 2 consists of selected strategies that focus on youth with elevated risk for significant difficulties (10–15 percent) and who are not responsive to universal approaches. Tier 3 refers to targeted strategies for a small (5–7 percent) proportion of students who experience significant risks, do not respond to Tiers 1 and 2, and need intensive supports that are individualized to address their specific intervention needs (Farmer, Sutherland, et al., 2016; Lane et al., 2015; Lewis, 2016; Maggin, Wehby, Farmer, and Brooks, 2016).

General conceptions of MTSS models suggest that Tiers 1 and 2 consist of research-proven, evidence-based practices that follow a manualized protocol that is designed to be implemented in a standardized approach with fidelity (Cook and Odom, 2013; Danielson and Rosenquist, 2014). In contrast, Tier 3 tends to involve individualized approaches that build from evidence-based practices but use data, experimentation, and the careful matching of interventions to the individual needs and responses of specific students (Fuchs and Fuchs, 2015; Kern and Wehby, 2014; Ludlow, 2014).

Although the MTSS framework is in some ways consistent with a dynamic systems perspective, the two approaches differ somewhat in terms of focus and scope. These differences are complementary rather than contradictory, and the two perspectives may be combined to enhance the content and delivery of services for students who need intensive supports (Farmer, Sutherland, et al., 2016; Maggin et al., 2016).

There are three primary differences between current MTSS frameworks and the dynamic systems perspective. First, MTSS focuses on students' responses to intervention and does not take into consideration developmental data or individual difference factors that may dynamically affect responses to specific interventions. In contrast, the dynamic systems perspective aligns more strongly with the Institute of Medicine's (1994) tiered framework of universal (Tier 1), selected (Tier 2), and targeted (Tier 3) levels of support where the focus is on the level of risk experienced by youth.

Second, in the MTSS model the focus is on standardized interventions in the first two tiers, and individualization and intensification do not occur until Tier 3. From a dynamic systems perspective, there may be a need to adapt specific strategies within all three tiers. Third, building from previous points, MTSS centers on identifying effective interventions and involves sifting through progressively more intensive strategies until the desired outcome is achieved. The dynamic systems perspective suggests a different vantage point and centers on reducing risk and promoting adaptation within each tier of support.

It is possible to merge the MTSS and dynamic systems perspectives to better support the intensification of intervention for students with LD. At Tier 1, MTSS involves implementing evidence-based strategies practices that are empirically proven to be effective with the general population, while a dynamic systems perspective focuses on promoting the success of all students. Both are universal. For MTSS the universal aspect is the strategy. For the dynamic systems perspective, the universal aspect is the target population, which is all students. These perspectives can be combined and universal evidence-based practices should be used.

For students who experience risk, however, there may be a need to adapt the practices in some way such as changing the format, the timing of how it is presented, or considering how the context may be altered to enhance the student's response to it. At Tier 2, MTSS involves providing more intensive support for small groups of students who do not respond to Tier 1, whereas from a dynamic systems perspective the goal is help the student develop stronger skills and competencies in the domain of difficulty while also providing supports that prevent additional risks from developing.

The MTSS approach uses more tailored evidence-based practices, but it should be done with a careful eye toward person-in-context factors; grouping students who support each other's difficulties should be avoided (Dishion and Snyder, 2005). Further, efforts to reinforce students' strengths and competencies should not be neglected (i.e., do not focus only on remediating the problem). At Tier 3, both approaches focus on youth who experience significant difficulties.

From an MTSS perspective, these are students who are not responsive to standard evidence-based practices, while from a dynamic systems perspective these are students who are experiencing multiple risks that collectively contribute to the difficulties they experience. Both perspectives suggest that intervention should be individualized. We suggest that the data-driven framework of MTSS should be combined with a focus on promoting the developmental systems reorganization of the various risks the student is experiencing

(Farmer and Farmer, 2001; Farmer et al., 2017; Farmer, Sutherland, et al., 2016).

The MTSS and the dynamic systems perspectives can be merged to enhance the outcomes for all youth. The adaptation of interventions can occur across all three tiers of intervention and as adaptations are made in Tiers 1 and 2 they should be recorded and the information used to guide further intensification at the Tier 3 level. Response to intervention information should be augmented with profiles of school adjustment factors as well as person-in-context data. When this is done, interventions can be strengthened for students with LD.

The concept of intervention intensification and the implications of a dynamic systems perspective for implementing tailored, data-driven strategies that are individualized to students' specific strengths and needs must be part of the discussion.

INTERVENTION INTENSIFICATION AND THE DYNAMIC SYSTEMS PERSPECTIVE

The points discussed previously should be considered through the lens of promoting academic, behavioral, and social success for students requiring more intensive support. In this case, the focus is on students at the Tier 3 level of support via the provision of targeted, individualized intensive interventions for those students with the most persistent and severe academic, behavioral, and social needs (Farmer, Sutherland, et al., 2016; Lane et al., 2015; Ludlow, 2014).

Following a discussion of intervention intensification within dynamic systems, with a particular focus on the influence of peers and teacher-student interactions, a brief example will be given that illustrates how a teacher intensifies intervention while taking into account the influence of peers and her own behavior.

Intervention Intensification

For students within MTSS who are not responding to Tier 1 and 2 interventions, there has been a growing emphasis on functional behavioral assessment (FBA) and data-based individualization (DBI) at the Tier 3 level of MTSS. The goal of functional assessment is to determine the proximal contextual factors that evoke and reinforce problem behavior, to adapt the environment in ways that reduce the likelihood of the recurrence of the problem behavior, to teach adaptive behaviors that replace the problem behavior, and to reinforce the occurrence of the adaptive behavior (O'Neill, Albin, Storey, Horner, and Sprague, 2015).

When intensifying intervention from Tier 2 levels of support, DBI guides teachers in making more informed instructional decisions. DBI is a continual process in which the teacher uses progress monitoring to determine a student's performance within a given intervention (Danielson and Rosenquist, 2014). Once initial progress monitoring is complete, the teacher will use these data to make a decision to intensify the intervention (e.g., smaller group size, increased dosage). Progress monitoring is again used to evaluate the effectiveness of the intensification, another decision point is reached in which the teacher must determine whether to maintain the intensification or alter the intervention.

Intensifying Intervention within Dynamic Systems: Influences of Peers and Teachers

The dynamic systems perspective involves clarifying how multiple factors and processes contribute to human functioning and outcomes (Cairns, 2000; Sameroff, 2000; Smith and Thelen, 2003)—in this case, students' academic, behavioral, and social functioning. Differing from the MTSS perspective, the dynamic systems perspective suggests and takes into account that students needing Tier 3 supports are experiencing multiple risks that collectively contribute to the difficulties they experience.

The data-driven framework of MTSS (e.g., FBA, DBI), therefore, should be combined with a focus on promoting the developmental systems reorganization of the various risks the student is experiencing (Farmer and Farmer, 2001; Farmer et al., 2017; Farmer, Sutherland, et al., 2016). An important context within which developmental systems reorganization can take place is the classroom.

The next focus is on two important factors within the classroom that should be considered in order to maximize the effectiveness of intensified interventions: peer relationships and teacher-student interactions. First, social interactional theory provides a useful framework for understanding how classroom contexts contribute to the behavioral adjustment of students with LD who have intensive learning and behavioral needs.

According to this perspective, children's social behavior is established and maintained through the complex coordination and adaptation of individual and contextual influences during social interchanges with teachers and peers (Cairns, 1997). From this vantage point, the immediate controls of the actions of a child rest in the behavior of the other person or persons involved in the interaction (Sears, 1951). Social actions, however, are multidetermined and involve the coactive contributions of neurobiological, endocrinological, cognitive, social network, and cultural factors (Cairns, 1979; Gottlieb, 1996).

During social interactions, therefore, there is an ongoing calibration between the propensities of the self and the demands of others (Cairns, 2000).

This means that a student's internal capacities (e.g., social cognitive skills, activity rates, and emotional and behavioral regulation) and the characteristics of her or his social context (e.g., peer groups, available social roles, social norms) influence each other as they collectively contribute to the development of distinct patterns of social behaviors and skills (Farmer, Magee-Quinn, Hussey, and Holahan, 2001).

For many students with intensive intervention needs, their social patterns are likely to reflect skill deficits including social information processing problems, difficulties regulating the rate and intensity of social behavior, and attentional difficulties (Gresham and MacMillan, 1997; Nowicki, 2003; Swanson and Malone, 1992; Vaughn, McIntosh, and Spencer-Rowe, 1991). How these difficulties are expressed and maintained in the classroom depends in large part on the social structures, social roles, and peer-group dynamics that underlie children's social interactions (Farmer, Pearl, and Van Acker, 1996).

When a student is viewed by others as being a leader, bully, victim, good student, poor student, or some other social role, classmates and teachers are likely to interact with the student in ways that are specific to her or his social role or reputation. Consequently, the collective expectations and interactions patterns of classmates and teachers may support and sustain the student's social role and her or his behavior.

Although peers clearly exert great influence on students' problem behavior in the classroom, as part of the classroom context the teacher also has an enormous amount of influence on establishing, maintaining, and reinforcing social norms (Hendrickx et al. 2016). At the same time, the characteristics of the students in a teacher's classroom will impact her/his ability to maintain an appropriate learning climate. Students who exhibit chronic problem behavior are likely to be treated differently by teachers than students who are typically compliant, and these teacher-student interactions may set the stage for an increased likelihood of problematic behavior (Gest and Rodkin, 2011).

Teacher-student interactions have been described as transactional in nature, whereby teacher and student behavior reciprocally influences each other over time (Sameroff, 2009; Sutherland and Oswald, 2005). Research indicates that increased positive interactions between teachers and students who typically display problem behavior can not only improve student behavior but also improve student engagement in instruction (Sutherland, Wehby, and Copeland, 2000; Cook et al., 2017).

To illustrate, Skinner and Belmont (1993) found that students who were more engaged in the classroom received more positive teacher behaviors, while students who were less engaged experienced more neglect and coercion from teachers and were treated with less consistency. Thus, teachers tended to promote further classroom engagement of students who were already engaged, and interacted with disengaged students in a way that increased the likelihood of further disengagement.

Skinner and Belmont (1993) describe these effects as magnificatory; that is, positive student engagement elicits positive teacher behavior, further eliciting student engagement, while the relative absence of student engagement elicits negative teacher behavior, further eliciting student disengagement. Therefore, if students and teachers affect each other's behavior in a reciprocal manner, it is reasonable to hypothesize that students' levels of engagement will predict the quantity, and quality, of teacher interactions that they encounter in the future.

Students who are engaged in the classroom, or who are perceived by teachers to be engaged, are likely to be treated differently than students who are not engaged. This differential treatment, while perhaps unwitting on the part of the teacher, may yield increased exposure to academic material, increased rates of opportunities to respond, superior task quality, and increased positive teacher attention for students exhibiting desired classroom behavior.

Meanwhile, less-engaged and disruptive/aggressive students are likely to receive less exposure to academic material, inferior task quality, and more negative and coercive attention.

Given the role that classroom contexts, and peers and teachers in particular, play in either limiting or promoting disruptive behavior and learning, it is critical that implementation of intensified interventions take into account both teacher and peer factors, as ignoring one might have extremely detrimental effects on treatment efficacy. Rodkin and Hodges (2003), for example, point out children may accept, but not internalize, adult-generated rules regarding problem behaviors such as bullying and aggression.

In this case, ignoring the influence of peers would limit the effectiveness of an otherwise well-meaning intervention (i.e., posted rules and expectations for classroom behavior); therefore, the ways that teachers can use their knowledge of classroom social dynamics to maximize intervention effectiveness with students with intensive needs is highly dependent on the particular circumstances of the individual needs of the student and the degree to which there is an adaptive and supportive classroom social structure. The example that follows illustrates a teacher using her knowledge of dynamic systems to provide intensive interventions with MTSS.

Integration of Dynamic Systems and Intensification of Intervention

Teachers may use the FBA process and DBI, in conjunction with their own assessments of peer social networks and support for problem behavior, to design interventions that have a greater likelihood of both affecting change in problem behavior and learning, as well as strengthening the maintenance of behavior change. Behavior change is more likely to be maintained over time if the classroom context (e.g., peer support, teacher-student interactions) is manipulated, providing students with natural reinforcers for their appropriate behavior.

To illustrate, Ms. Johnson, a third-grade teacher, was concerned that James's problem behavior was interfering with both his learning and that of his peers, and that she was spending an inordinate amount of time providing him with reprimands. James had not been responsive to Ms. Johnson's Tier 1 instruction and, in conjunction with the help of Ms. Townsend, the school counselor, she had made some Tier 2 accommodations (e.g., token economy) that had also not been successful. She then elicited the help of Ms. Townsend to conduct an FBA.

Their first step involved operationally defining the problem behavior, and they decided on an observable, measurable behavior: "During whole group instruction, James often calls out inappropriately, even after being given directions to raise a quiet hand." They next collected several forms of data, including (a) examining James's school records, (b) interviewing his mother, (c) completing a Problem Behavior Questionnaire (Lewis, Scott, and Sugai, 1994), and (d) observing James's behavior in both reading and math in order to document rates of Ms. Johnson's behaviors (e.g., opportunities to respond, praise, reprimands) toward James. These data forms are common to the FBA process and are often helpful in identifying possible functions of the problem behavior.

In addition to the above data, Ms. Townsend performed two additional tasks. First, she asked Ms. Johnson to (a) identify the students that James tends to hang around with most often, and (b) identify the most socially prominent students in the classroom. When she observed James's behavior during both reading and math, Ms. Townsend collected data on the occurrence of the problem behavior, as well as antecedents and consequences to the behavior (including Ms. Johnson's behaviors toward James), in order to determine if there was a pattern of antecedents or reinforcement.

At the same time, she also collected data on the peer responses to James's behavior, namely that of his closest friends as well as the more prominent students in the class. After collecting the data, the teacher and the counselor hypothesized that James's problem behavior was maintained by attention, both from his teacher and from peers. The data indicated that when James called out inappropriately, Ms. Johnson frequently would reprimand him, providing him with teacher attention.

Ms. Townsend also observed that in the minutes following James's undesirable behavior, Ms. Johnson would miss opportunities to either call on him when he appropriately sought attention or reward him for meeting behavioral expectations. Additionally, on approximately 50 percent of the occurrences of problem behavior, peers—both his closest friends as well as the prominent members of the class—supported his problem behavior by laughing and giggling, as well as looking at him and making faces.

In light of the data from the FBA, including the teacher's knowledge of the peer networks in the classroom, Ms. Johnson and Ms. Townsend agreed upon several intervention strategies to support James's prosocial behavior. First, they identified the replacement behavior: raising a quiet hand. Ms. Johnson would make an effort to explicitly state her expectations of this behavior at the beginning of each lesson, also providing prompts when necessary.

To address James's need for her attention, she would attempt to ignore his call-outs, instead providing a prompt for him (e.g., raising her own hand), then immediately calling on him when he complied. In addition, she would attempt to increase her positive attention to James (i.e., praise) when he performed the target behavior, monitoring her own behavior using self-evaluation. Finally, to address the peer supports for problem behavior, Ms. Johnson and Ms. Townsend agreed upon two strategies.

First, James's seating arrangement was changed, moving him to the front of the class, several seats away from both his closest friend and the more prominent students, creating a physical arrangement that made peer attention more difficult. Second, Ms. Johnson would attempt to quickly quell peer support for the problem behavior with gentle reprimands, as well as providing reinforcement for students who ignored the inappropriate behavior. Over a period of several days, with diligent adherence to the intervention, data collection indicated a significant increase in James's hand raises, increasing the instructional time for all students in the classroom.

FINAL THOUGHTS

Multiple influences contribute to the academic, behavioral, and social success of students with LD, and these influences may be particularly salient for students with LD not responsive to Tier 1 and 2 supports within MTSS. The dynamic systems perspective can help explain how these influences work to either promote or impede student academic, behavioral, and social development, informing intervention intensification at the Tier 3 level of support.

Two classroom factors—peer social networks and teacher-student interactions—clearly exert a great deal of influence not only on the classroom behavior of students but also on downstream developmental outcomes. Through a heightened awareness of these complex factors and how they influence each other, teachers can move toward becoming more adept at manipulating the social context in ways that will increase the likelihood of success of intensified interventions for our most vulnerable students.

POINTS TO REMEMBER

- *The Multi-Tiered System of Supports (MTSS) is ubiquitous in schools; the impact of MTSS may be increased through a better understanding of dynamic systems and multiple influences on students' development.*
- *There are many influences on the developmental trajectory of students, such as family, biology, school, and community. Teachers have limited influence over many of these factors; one context where teachers elicit great influence, however, is within the classroom.*
- *By taking a dynamic systems perspective, teachers can better understand how multiple factors work in concert to influence students' academic, behavioral, and social development.*
- *Through understanding how these factors work together, teachers can better design intervention approaches within MTSS to meet the needs of students with intensive learning and behavior needs.*
- *Teachers who demonstrate an understanding of how peer contexts within the classroom as well as their own interaction patterns influence student behavior are going to have greater success implementing interventions at each of the three levels of MTSS.*

The primary author can be reached at kssuther@vcu.edu.

NOTE

Correspondence concerning this chapter should be addressed to Kevin S. Sutherland, Department of Counseling and Special Education, School of Education, Virginia Commonwealth University, 1015 W. Main St., PO Box 842020, Richmond, VA 23284. Internet mail may be sent to kssuther@vcu.edu. This was supported in part by research grant R305A150246 from the Institute of Education Sciences to Kevin S. Sutherland and research grants (R305A120812; R305A140434) from the Institute of Education Sciences to Thomas W. Farmer. It was also supported in part by Grant H325H140001 from the US Department of Education, Office of Special Education Programs (OSEP). The views expressed in this chapter are those of the authors and do not represent the granting agencies.

REFERENCES

Ahn, H.-J., and Rodkin, P. C. (2014). Classroom-level predictors of the social status of aggression: Friendship centralization, friendship density, teacher–student attunement, and gender. *Journal of Educational Psychology,* 106, 1144–55. https://doi.org/10.1037/a0036091.

Al-Yagon, M. (2016). Perceived close relationships with parents, teachers, and peers: Predictors of social, emotional, and behavioral features in adolescents with LD or comorbid LD and ADHD. *Journal of Learning Disabilities,* 49, 597–615. https://doi.org/10.1177/00222 19415620569.

Bergman, L. R., and Vargha, A. (2013). Matching method to problem: A developmental science perspective. *European Journal of Developmental Psychology,* 10, 9–28. https://doi:10.1080/17405629.2012.732920.

Bronfenbrenner, U. (1996). Foreword. In R. B. Cairns, G. H. Elder, and E. J. Costello (eds.), *Developmental science* (pp. ix–xvii). New York: Cambridge University Press.

———. (2005). *Making human beings human: Bioecological perspectives on human development.* Thousand Oaks, CA: Sage.

Cairns, R. B. (1979). *Social development: The origins and plasticity of interchanges.* San Francisco: W. H. Freeman.

———. (2000). Developmental science: Three audacious implications. In L. R. Bergman, R. B. Cairns, L-G. Nilsson, and L. Nystedt (eds.), *Developmental science and the holistic approach* (pp. 49–62). Mahwah, NJ: Lawrence Erlbaum.

Cairns, R. B., and Cairns, B. D. (1994). *Lifelines and risks: Pathways of youth in our time.* New York: Harvester Wheatsheaf.

Cook, B. G., and Odom, S. L. (2013). Evidence-based practices and implementation science in special education. *Exceptional Children,* 79, 135–44. https://doi.org/10.1177/0014402913 07900201.

Cook, C. R., Grady, E. A., Long, A. C., Renshaw, T., Codding, R. S., Fiat, A., and Larson, M. (2017). Evaluating the impact of increasing general education teachers' ratio of positive-to-negative interactions on students' classroom behavior. *Journal of Positive Behavior Interventions,* 19(2), 67–77. https://doi.org/10.1177/1098300716679137.

Danielson, L., and Rosenquist, C. (2014). Introduction to the TEC special issue on data-based individualization. *Teaching Exceptional Children,* 46(4), 6–12. https://doi.org/10.1177/00 40059914522965.

Dishion, T. J., and Snyder, J. (2004). An introduction to the special issue on advances in process and dynamic system analysis of social interaction and the development of antisocial behavior. *Journal of Abnormal Child Psychology,* 32, 575–78.

England, M. J., Butler, A. S., and Gonzalez, M. L. (2015). *Psychosocial interventions for mental and substance use disorders: A framework for establishing evidence-based standards.* Washington, DC: National Academies Press.

Farmer, T. W. (2013). When universal approaches and prevention services are not enough: The importance of understanding the stigmatization of special education for students with EBD. *Behavioral Disorders,* 39, 32–42. https://doi.org/10.1177/019874291303900105.

Farmer, T. W., Dawes, M., Hamm, J. V., Lee, D., Mehtaji, M., Hoffman, A. S., and Brooks, D. S. (2017). Classroom social dynamics management: Why the invisible hand of the teacher matters for special education. *Remedial and Special Education.* https://doi.org/10.1177/0741932517718359.

Farmer, T. W., and Farmer, E. M. Z. (2001). Developmental science, systems of care, and prevention of emotional and behavioral problems in youth. *American Journal of Orthopsychiatry,* 71, 171–81. Retrieved from https://www.ncbi.nlm.nih.gov/pubmed/11347359.

Farmer, T. W., Gatzke-Kopp, L. M., Lee, D. L., Dawes, M., and Talbott, E. (2016). Research and policy on disability: Linking special education to developmental science. *Policy Insights from the Behavioral and Brain Sciences,* 3, 138–45. https://doi.org/10.1177/23727322 15624217.

Farmer, T. W., Magee-Quinn, M., Hussey, W., and Holahan, T. (2001). The development of disruptive behavior disorders and correlated constraints: Implications for intervention. *Behavioral Disorders,* 26, 117–30. https://doi.org/10.1177/019874290102600202.

Farmer, T. W., Pearl, R., and Van Acker, R. M. (1996). Expanding the social skills deficit framework: A developmental synthesis perspective, classroom social networks, and implications for the social growth of students with disabilities. *Journal of Special Education,* 30, 232–56. https://doi.org/10.1177/002246699603000302.

Farmer, T. W., Reinke, W., and Brooks, D. S. (2014). Managing classrooms and challenging behavior: Theoretical considerations and critical issues. *Journal of Emotional and Behavioral Disorders,* 22, 67–73. https://doi.org/10.1177/1063426614522693.

Farmer, T. W., Rodkin, P. C., Pearl, R., and Van Acker, R. (1999). Teacher-assessed behavioral configurations, peer-assessments, and self-concepts of elementary students with mild disabilities. *Journal of Special Education,* 33, 66–80.

Farmer, T. W., Sutherland, K. S., Talbott, E., Brooks, D., Norwalk, K., and Huneke, M. (2016). Special educators as intervention specialists: Dynamic systems and the complexity of intensifying intervention for students with emotional and behavioral disorders. *Journal of Emotional and Behavioral Disorders,* 24, 173–86. https://doi.org/10.1177/1063426616650166.

Frederickson, N. L., and Furnham, A. F. (2004). Peer-assessed behavioural characteristics and sociometric rejection: Differences between pupils who have moderate learning difficulties and their mainstream peers. *British Journal of Educational Psychology,* 74, 391–410. https://doi.org/10.1177/002246699903300201.

Fuchs, D., and Fuchs, L. S. (2015). Rethinking service delivery for students with significant learning problems: Developing and implementing intensive interventions. *Remedial and Special Education,* 36, 105–11. https://doi.org/10.1177/0741932514558337.

Fuchs, L. S., Fuchs, D., and Compton, D. L. (2012). Intervention effects for students with comorbid forms of learning disability: Understanding the needs of non-responders. *Journal of Learning Disabilities,* 46, 534–48. https://doi.org/10.1177/0022219412468889.

Gest, S. D., and Rodkin, P. C. (2011). Teaching practices and elementary classroom peer ecologies. *Journal of Applied Developmental Psychology,* 32, 288–96. http://dx.doi.org/10.1016/j.appdev.2011.02.004.

Gresham, F. M., and MacMillan, D. L. (1997). Social competence and affective characteristics of students with mild disabilities. *Review of Educational Research,* 67, 377–415. https://doi.org/10.3102/00346543067004377.

Gottlieb, G. (1996). Developmental psychobiological theory. In R. B. Cairns, G. H. Elder Jr., and E. J. Costello (eds.), *Developmental science* (pp. 63–77). New York: Cambridge University Press.

Hendrickx, M. M., Mainhard, M. T., Boor-Klip, H. J., Cillessen, A. H., and Brekelmans, M. (2016). Social dynamics in the classroom: Teacher support and conflict and the peer ecology. *Teaching and Teacher Education,* 53, 30–40. Retrieved from http://www.sciencedirect.com/science/article/pii/S0742051X15300135.

Kern, L., and Wehby, J. H. (2014). Using data to intensify behavioral interventions for individual students. *Teaching Exceptional Children,* 46, 45–53. https://doi.org/10.1177/0040059914522970.

Kunnen, S. E. (2012). *A dynamic systems approach to adolescent development.* New York: Routledge.

Lane, K. L., Carter, E. W., Jenkins, A., Dwiggins, L., and Germer, K. (2015). Supporting comprehensive, integrated, three-tiered models of prevention in schools: Administrators perspectives. *Journal of Positive Behavior Interventions,* 17, 209–22. https://doi.org/10.1177/1098300715578916.

Lewis, T. J. (2016). Does the field of EBD need a distinct set of "intensive" interventions or more systemic intensity within a continuum of social/emotional supports? *Journal of Emotional and Behavioral Disorders,* 24(3), 187–90. https://doi.org/10.1177/1063426616652866.

Lewis, T. J., Scott, T. M., and Sugai, G. (1994). The problem behavior questionnaire: A teacher-based instrument to develop functional hypotheses of problem behavior in general education classrooms. *Assessment for Effective Intervention,* 19(2–3), 103–15. https://doi.org/10.1177/073724779401900207.

Ludlow, B. (2014). Intensifying intervention: Kicking it up a notch. *Teaching Exceptional Children,* 46, 4. https://doi.org/10.1177/0040059914523762.

Maggin, D. M., Wehby, J. H., Farmer, T. W., and Brooks, D. S. (2016). Intensive interventions for students with emotional and behavioral disorders: Issues, theory, and future directions. *Journal of Emotional and Behavioral Disorders,* 24, 127–37. https://doi.org/10.1177/1063426616661498.

Magnusson, D., and Cairns, R. B. (1996). Developmental science: Principles and illustrations. In R. B. Cairns, G. H. Elder Jr, and E. J. Costello (eds)., *Developmental science* (pp. 7–30). New York: Cambridge University Press.

Nowicki, E. A. (2003). A meta-analysis of the social competence of children with learning disabilities compared to classmates of low and average to high achievement. *Learning Disability Quarterly, 26*, 171–88. https://doi.org/10.2307/1593650.

O'Neill, R. E., Albin, R. W., Storey, K., Horner, R. H., and Sprague, J. R. (2015). *Functional assessment and program development for challenging behavior: A practical handbook.* Stamford, CT: Cengage Learning.

Rodkin, P. C., and Hodges, E. V. E. (2003). Bullies and victims in the peer ecology: Four questions for psychologists and school professionals. *School Psychology Review, 32*(3), 384–400. Retrieved from https://eric.ed.gov/?id=EJ823561.

Roeser, R. W., and Peck, S. C. (2003). Patterns and pathways of educational achievement across adolescence: A holistic-developmental perspective. *New Directions for Child and Adolescent Development, 101*, 39–62. Retrieved from https://eric.ed.gov/?id=EJ773051.

Sameroff, A. J. (2000). Developmental systems and psychopathology. *Development and Psychopathology, 12*, 297–312. Retrieved from https://www.ncbi.nlm.nih.gov/pubmed/11014740.

———, ed. (2009). *The transactional model of development: How children and contexts shape each other.* Washington, DC: American Psychological Association.

Samuels, C. A. (2016). What are multifaceted systems of support. *Ed Week.* Retrieved from http://www.edweek.org/ew/articles/2016/12/14/what-are-multitiered-systems-of-supports.html.

Sears, R. R. (1951). A theoretical framework for personality and social behavior. *American Psychologist, 6*, 476–83. Retrieved from https://www.researchgate.net/publication/232468180_A_theoretical_framework_for_personality_and_social_behavior.

Shores, R. E., and Wehby, J. H. (1999). Analyzing social behavior of children with emotional and behavioral disorders in classrooms. *Journal of Emotional and Behavioral Disorders, 7*, 194–99. https://doi.org/10.1177/106342669900700401.

Skinner, E. A., and Belmont, M. J. (1993). Motivation in the classroom: Reciprocal effects of teacher behavior and student engagement across the school year. *Journal of Educational Psychology, 85*, 571–81. Retrieved from https://eric.ed.gov/?id=EJ476869.

Smith, L. B., and Thelen, E. (2003). Development as a dynamic system. *Trends in Cognitive Sciences, 7*, 343–48. Retrieved from https://www.ncbi.nlm.nih.gov/pubmed/12907229.

Sutherland, K. S., and Oswald, D. (2005). The relationship between teacher and student behavior in classrooms for students with emotional and behavioral disorders: Transactional processes. *Journal of Child and Family Studies, 14*, 1–14. Retrieved from https://www.researchgate.net/publication/225830898_The_Relationship_Between_Teacher_and_Student_Behavior_in_Classrooms_for_Students_with_Emotional_and_Behavioral_Disorders_Transactional_Processes.

Sutherland, K. S., Wehby, J. H., and Copeland, S. R. (2000). Effect of varying rates of behavior specific praise on the on-task behavior of students with emotional and behavioral disorders. *Journal of Emotional and Behavioral Disorders, 8*, 2–8, 26. https://doi.org/10.1177/106342660000800101.

Swanson, H. L., and Malone, S. (1992). Social skills and learning disabilities: A meta-analysis the literature. *School Psychology Review, 21*, 427–43. Retrieved from https://www.researchgate.net/publication/232520653_Social_skills_and_learning_disabilities_A_meta-analysis_of_the_literature.

Vallance, D. D., Cummings, R. L., and Humphries, T. (1998). Mediators of the risk for problem behavior in children with language learning disabilities. *Journal of Learning Disabilities, 31*, 160–71. https://doi.org/10.1177/002221949803100206.

Vaughn, S., McIntosh, R., and Spencer-Rowe, J. (1991). Peer rejection is a stubborn thing: Increasing peer acceptance of rejected students with learning disabilities. *Learning Disabilities Research and Practice, 6*, 83–88. Retrieved from https://eric.ed.gov/?id=EJ428548.

Chapter Three

Evidence-based Instructional Practices and Models to Assist Students with Learning Disabilities

Nicholas D. Young, *American International College,* and Kristen Bonanno-Sotiropoulos, *Bay Path University*

The goal of providing high-quality instruction is of the utmost importance for students with learning disabilities. Determining and implementing evidence-based instructional practices is a key piece of the Individuals with Disabilities Act (2004) as well as several other important pieces of legislation. Teachers must be deemed highly qualified and licensed according to state and federal law. Additionally, educators must consistently identify and implement strategies to encourage learning despite the learning struggles of students (Maheady, Rafferty, Patti, and Budin, 2016).

A critical component of both the Individuals with Disabilities Education Improvement Act of 2004 as well as the Every Student Succeeds Act of 2015 (Klein, 2016) is the emphasis on the use of research-based or evidence-based instructional practices. Research strongly suggests that implementation of evidence-based instructional practices works to close the achievement gap by optimizing student outcomes (Cook, Tankersley, Cook, and Landrum, 2008; Scheeler, Budin, and Markelz, 2016). Practices that have been proven effective through widespread research are considered to be evidence based. However, there are criteria standards in place to determine the degree of labeling that a practice can receive (Council for Exceptional Children, 2014).

According to the US Department of Education's Institute of Educational Sciences and the National Center for Education Evaluation and Regional Assistance (2003), not all practitioners have been trained on how to identify practices considered to be evidence based. This presents a disconnect between the training of all teachers and the expectations in the field. Literature suggests there are several strategies that higher education institutions, specifically teacher preparation programs, can develop to address this disconnect (Scheeler et al., 2016).

In addition to the use of evidence-based instructional practices, the Individuals with Disabilities Education Improvement Act of 2004 (IDEIA) clearly states,

> to the maximum extent appropriate, children with disabilities, including children in public or private institutions or other care facilities, are educated with children who are not disabled, and special classes, separate schooling, or other removal of children with disabilities from the regular educational environment occurs only when the nature or severity of the disability of a child is such that education in regular classes with the use of supplementary aids and services cannot be achieved satisfactorily. (US Department of Education, 2004)

Here, children with exceptionalities are entitled to receive special education services in the least restrictive environment (LRE), which in many cases is the general education classroom. Children with exceptionalities may bring a diverse set of needs, challenges, and dynamics into the general education classroom. This mandate presents a dire need for educators to be fluent in evidence-based instructional strategies and models.

On the other end of the spectrum, these children also bring opportunities for disability awareness, learning opportunities, and can secure collaboration efforts. With the increase in the number of students with exceptionalities receiving services in the inclusive setting, the establishment of effective partnerships between general education teachers, special education teachers, and related service providers is not only necessary but is required. Evidence-based strategies and models are available to support students with learning disabilities within inclusion classrooms: differentiated instruction, co-teaching models, direct and explicit teaching, a Universal Design for Learning framework, as well as peer-mediated instruction.

EVIDENCE-BASED INSTRUCTION PRACTICES

Contributions of Federal Regulations

Federal regulations, including the Individuals with Disabilities Education Improvement Act of 2004 (IDEIA) and the Every Student Succeeds Act (2015), mandate the use of evidence-based practices, also referred to as scientifically based, in order to provide the best learning opportunities for students with disabilities. The identification and implementation of evidence-based special education practices work to close the achievement gap by optimizing student outcomes (Cook et al., 2008; Scheeler et al., 2016).

Unfortunately, not all practitioners have been trained on how to identify practices considered to be evidence based, and this presents a disconnect between the training of special education teachers and the expectations in the field (US Department of Education, Institute of Educational Sciences, and the National Center for Education Evaluation and Regional Assistance, 2003).

Determination of Evidence-based Special Education Practices

Producing positive student outcomes within a well-defined area—in addition to being specific to a particular population of students—is needed for an intervention to be evidence based (Cook et al., 2008). Extensive research has been conducted in order to clarify specific criteria for labeling a strategy, intervention, and/or practice as evidence based (Council for Exceptional Children, 2014).

Research conducted through randomized control trials, comparison groups, and single-subject designs are a good starting point for identifying the effectiveness of an intervention (Council for Exceptional Children, 2014; Cook et al.; US Department of Education, Institute of Educational Sciences, 2003). It is important that the evidence collected from the studies identifies such things as the types of participants, the difference(s) between the control group and the intervention group, and the qualifications of the individual(s) who conducted the study, as well as the impact on future research (US Department of Education, Institute of Educational Sciences, 2003).

The Council for Exceptional Children developed a set of quality indicators for meeting the criteria for an evidence-based practice. These quality indicators include the context and setting in which the study was conducted; the participants in the study; a thorough description of the intervention; confirmation that the study was conducted with fidelity, including internal validity, outcome measures, and variables; and information on how the data was collected and analyzed (Council for Exceptional Children, 2014).

Supporting Students with Learning Disabilities: Classroom Models and Strategies of Differentiated Instruction

One of the many advantages of differentiated instruction is its ability to provide learning opportunities for all students within the general education classroom (Ford, 2013). Differentiated instruction refers to a flexible approach to teaching that considers the content, the learning process, learning styles, presentation strategies, and assessment techniques to provide students with the structure to maximize strengths, accommodate for weaknesses, and provide for timely remediation (Ministry of Education and British Columbia School Superintendent's Association, 2011).

Scruggs, Mastropieri, and Marshak (2012) define differentiated instruction as supplying students with instructional strategies and materials that meet their individual learning needs. Obiakor, Harris, Mutua, Rotatori, and Algozzine (2012) add that both general education and special education teachers, through collaboration, must provide flexibility in their teaching approaches as well as in the curriculum to support differentiated instruction.

Tomlinson (2014), a well-known author on differentiated instruction, highlights several key aspects of differentiation. First, teachers must be flexible in the way they engage students in the learning process. Teachers must acknowledge and account for learning interests and styles. Secondly, teachers must provide alternatives for learning, both input and output. In other words, teachers must provide options for presenting the content and options for ways that students can show comprehension of the knowledge. Finally, teachers must use their time wisely, use flexibility in choosing instructional strategies, and form partnerships with their students in order to create and maintain a positive learning environment that supports teaching and learning.

Effective differentiated instruction incorporates several components: first, clarification of all concepts and generalizations; second, the use of assessments as a teaching tool to guide instruction and learning, and not only as a measure; third, inclusion of critical and creative thinking as a goal in every lesson; fourth, assurance that every student is engaged in the learning process; and lastly, a balance of tasks between teacher-assigned tasks and student-chosen assignments (Tomlinson, 2014).

Co-Teaching

There continues to be an ongoing debate as to whether full inclusion is beneficial to meeting the academic needs of students with disabilities. Some researchers argue that to make inclusion effective there must be well-established and supporting collaboration between general education teachers and special education teachers (Sailor and Roger, 2005; Skrtic, Harris, and Shriner, 2005). On the other side, researchers such as Fuchs, Fuchs, and Stecker (2010) argue that full inclusion is simply not feasible or effective, especially at meeting the needs of students with learning disabilities.

One effective way to ensure successful inclusion practices is through the use of a co-teaching model. In co-teaching, a general education and special education teacher work together to plan, execute, and assess teaching and learning for all students (Solis, Vaughn, Swanson, and McCulley, 2012). According to Inclusive Classrooms Project (n.d.), there are six evidence-based models for implementing co-teaching: one teach, one assist; station teaching; parallel teaching; alternative teaching; and team teaching.

In the one teach, one assist model, one teacher is responsible for instructing all students while the other teacher provides ongoing support to all students. In the station teaching model, the students are divided up into groups, typically three groups. Each group has the opportunity to engage in small group instruction with one of the teachers and has the opportunity to participate in independent practice as well. In the parallel teaching model, the students are broken into two groups. Each teacher provides instruction to a smaller group of students (Ford, 2013).

The alternative teaching model incorporates one teacher instructing the students while the second teacher provides the preteaching instruction as well as any reteaching that might occur. Finally, in a team-teaching approach, both teachers provide instruction to the whole class. Both teachers take turns leading the instruction and modeling good student behavior and skills (Ford, 2013).

Direct and Explicit Instruction

Direct instruction, also referred to as explicit instruction, is an instructional strategy where a strategy, skill, or specific content is taught precisely by the teacher (Archer and Hughes, 2011). Direct instruction involves the teacher explaining and modeling a skill, concept, or strategy while providing guidance, feedback, and reinforcement (Archer and Hughes, 2011; Ministry of Education and British Columbia School Superintendent's Association, 2011). Effective differentiated instruction occurs when the following steps are followed.

First, the teacher must make sure that the students are aware and understand the learning goal in addition to the work that is expected. This step is known as the "anticipatory set." The next step, "statement of the objective," provides for a clear explanation of the learning objective. The third step, simply referred to as "input," is when the teacher verbally explains the skill, strategy, or task. Next, "modeling" encompasses the teacher modeling the skill/strategy along with guiding practice to develop the skill/strategy with the students. During this step, it is also helpful if the teacher provides examples and nonexamples of the skill/strategy (Archer and Hughes, 2011).

"Checking for understanding" consists of students engaging in self-evaluation. The teacher should first provide criteria guidance for the self-evaluation process. After the self-evaluation, in the next step, "guided and monitored practice and feedback," students participate in independent practice while the teacher provides support and feedback. The final step, "independent practice," allows for students to engage in activities to assist with building confidence and independence (Archer and Hughes, 2011; Ministry of Education and British Columbia School Superintendent's Association, 2011).

Universal Design for Learning

Universal Design for Learning (UDL) is a framework that combines research in the fields of neuroscience and education (Wiggins and McTighe, 2005). The framework allows the educator to design learning environments that enhance teaching and learning for all students. UDL is a proactive strategy for integrating supports and choices into the curriculum. UDL plans for the greatest range of needs within the classroom from the beginning; it is not an afterthought (Meyer, Rose, and Gordon, 2014). The UDL framework consists of three principles: multiple means of representation, multiple means of expression, and multiple means of engagement. In addition, respect for individual differences, learning styles, and personal attributes are embedded throughout the framework (Ministry of Education and British Columbia School Superintendent's Association, 2011).

Multiple means of representation ensure that educators provide various options for comprehension, language and math expressions, and perceptions. Examples include activating prior knowledge, highlighting big ideas and vocabulary, customizing the display of information, and emphasizing relationships.

Multiple means of expression provide options for executive functioning, expression and communication, and physical action. Examples include guiding and supporting goal setting, inclusion of multiple tools and media, providing scaffolded supports, and providing various methods for responding.

Multiple means of engagement support motivation for learning by providing options for self-regulation, sustaining effort, and building interest. Examples include setting high expectations, developing self-assessment and self-reflection skills, fostering collaboration and community, and providing individual choice (National Center on Universal Design for Learning, 2017).

Peer-Mediated Instruction

Peer-mediated instruction is an instructional model proven effective in inclusion classrooms and is well documented in the literature (Ford, 2013). Peer-mediated instruction incorporates students in the classroom taking on the role of teacher for students with disabilities. Peer instructors can provide two types of instruction: direct or indirect. Direct instruction is like tutoring, while indirect instruction occurs through peer modeling. One example of a well-known and frequently used elementary peer-mediated strategy is known as Peer-Assisted Learning Strategies, or simply P.A.L.S.

Using peer-mediated instruction, the teacher takes on the role of facilitator rather than the primary source of instruction. Obiakor et al. (2012) questions whether peer-mediated instruction is beneficial by itself. The authors suggest that the use of peer-mediated instruction is best when used in conjunction with other differentiated instruction or co-teaching strategies.

EVIDENCE-BASED INSTRUCTIONAL PRACTICES AND TEACHER PREPARATION PROGRAMS

Research, along with federal mandates, support the need for teacher preparation programs to expose teacher candidates to evidence-based instructional practices. First, both federal and state mandates—most notably, the Individuals with Disabilities Education Improvement Act, 2004 (IDEIA)—clearly states that teachers need to be trained in how to identify and implement evidence-based practices (Cook et al., 2008; Ideas That Work, n.d.).

Teacher candidates should be exposed to the use of evidence-based instructional practices through both theory and practice, resulting in well-informed practitioners once out in the field (Ficarra and Quinn, 2014). Teacher preparation programs must ensure that teacher candidates can select appropriate interventions and practices that are supported by empirical research and be able to implement the practice with fidelity (Scheeler et al., 2016).

Teachers who are well prepared, including exposure to the use of evidence-based practices, are more likely to remain in the field, thus creating stable educational environments that promote positive student outcomes (Boe, Shinn, and Cook, 2007; Ficarra and Quinn, 2014). Finally, increasing evidence shows that special education evidence-based practices implemented consistently and with fidelity improve student outcomes (Kretlow and Helf, 2013).

Challenges to Preparing Teacher Candidates on the Use of Evidence-Based Practices

Scheeler et al. (2016) identify six barriers to effective identification and implementation of special education evidence-based practices: insufficient preparation, lack of reinforcement, competing demands, lack of evidence-based culture, maintenance and generalization, and breadth of expertise. A closer examination of these barriers reveals the following insights. Qualitative surveys of higher education faculty confirm a lack of opportunities to employ special education evidence-based practices in field-based experiences, resulting in insufficient teacher preparation.

In addition, curriculum constraints do not offer much room for adequate practice in the use of evidence-based practices (Scheeler et al., 2016). Other research, again through qualitative surveys of preservice and licensed special education teachers, revealed limited exposure to evidence-based practices, infrequent use of evidence-based practices, and frequent use of practices with no empirical evidence. The absence of an evidence-based culture suggests that American public schools lack the guidance and fail to adopt and implement principles necessary for creating the use of evidence-based practices as the norm (Scheeler et al., 2016).

The Role of Evidence-Based Practices in Teacher Preparation Programs

There are several effective practices that teacher preparation programs should utilize to expose special education teacher candidates to evidence-based special education practices. Some of these practices include advanced faculty knowledge and modeling of evidence-based practices in coursework, the use of innovative tools, and the use of well-designed clinical experiences out in the field (Scheeler et al., 2016). A closer examination of these practices revealed details for implementation.

Faculty knowledge, as described by Scheeler et al. (2016), discusses the need for continuous learning, especially by college faculty in teacher preparation programs. The authors suggest that special education faculty focus their research efforts specifically on evidence-based practices within all academic areas. Another recommendation suggests creating a capstone project that involves having special education teacher candidates actively research, apply, and evaluate empirically based interventions (Scheeler et al., 2016).

Similarly, Mason-Williams, Frederick, and Mulcahy (2015) created a project that requires special education teacher candidates to identify the needs of a student, research and identify an empirically supported intervention, implement the strategy with fidelity, and collect progress-monitoring data. Modeling evidence-based practices in the college classroom is another critical way that teacher preparation programs can expose special education teacher candidates. Strategies such as peer or reciprocal teaching, providing immediate feedback, or student engagement strategies (including the use of clickers, response cards, or guided notes) are all examples of evidence-based strategies that can engage the adult learner (Scheeler et al., 2016).

FINAL THOUGHTS

The use of evidence-based instructional practices are not only mandated by federal legislation, but research has proven their effectiveness toward closing the achievement gap for students with disabilities (Cook et al., 2008; Scheeler et al., 2016). There are several evidence-based instructional models that have been identified as valuable for supporting inclusive practices, including co-teaching models, differentiated instruction, direct instruction, peer-mediated instruction, and the use of a Universal Design for Learning (UDL) framework (Ford, 2013; Meyer et al., 2014; Obiakor et al., 2012; Tomlinson, 2014).

It is critical that teacher candidates come into the field prepared to identify and implement evidence-based instructional practices within their classrooms (Cook et al., 2008). Scheeler et al. (2016) identified several practices that teacher preparation programs can employ to ensure that teacher candidates enter the field fully prepared. Some of these approaches include faculty modeling of evidence-based practices, the incorporation of well-designed clinical practicums, and evidence-based practices embedded throughout all coursework. Boe et al. (2007) assert that if teachers are well prepared to implement evidence-based instructional practices, they are more likely to stay in the field of education and, more importantly, make positive impacts on student achievement.

POINTS TO REMEMBER

- *The use of evidence-based instructional practices is critical to successful inclusive practices.*
- *The use of evidence-based instructional practices is mandated by federal education legislation.*
- *Research suggests that teachers are not leaving their teacher preparation programs fully prepared to implement evidence-based instructional practices.*
- *There are several approaches that teacher preparation programs can implement to ensure teachers are entirely prepared to utilize evidence-based practices in their classrooms.*
- *There are several evidence-based inclusive models that support students with disabilities: co-teaching, differentiated instruction, direct instruction, peer-mediated instruction, and universal design for learning.*

The primary author can be reached at nyoung1191@aol.com.

REFERENCES

Archer, A., and Hughes, C. (2011). *Explicit instruction: Effective and efficient teaching.* New York: Guilford Press.

Boe, E., Shinn, S., and Cook, L. H. (2007). Does teacher preparation matter for beginning teachers in either special or general education? *Journal of Special Education,* 41(3), 158–70. Retrieved from http://repository.upenn.edu/cgi/viewcontent.cgi?article=1190&context=gse_pubs.

Cook, B., Tankersley, M., Cook, L., and Landrum, T. (2008). Evidence-based practices in special education: Some practical considerations. *Intervention in School and Clinic Hammill Institute on Disabilities,* 44(2), 66–75. https://doi.org/10.1177/1053451208321452.

Council for Exceptional Children. (2014). *Standards for evidence-based practices in special education. Council for Exceptional Children.* Retrieved from http://www.cec.sped.org/~/media/Files/Standards/Evidence%20based%20Practices%20and%20Practice/EBP%20FINAL.pdf.

Ficarra, L., and Quinn, K. (2014). Teachers' facility with evidence-based classroom management practices: An investigation of teacher preparation programs and in-service conditions. *Journal of Teacher Education for Sustainability,* 16(2), 71–87. Retrieved from http://files.eric.ed.gov/fulltext/EJ1108117.pdf.

Ford, J. (2013). *Educating students with learning disabilities in inclusive classrooms.* Retrieved from http://corescholar.libraries.wright.edu/cgi/viewcontent.cgi?article=1154&context=ejie.

Fuchs, D., Fuchs, L., and Stecker, P. (2010). The blurring of special education in a new continuum of general education placements and services. *Exceptional Children,* 76, 301–23. https://doi.org/10.1177/001440291007600304.

Ideas That Work. (n.d.). Evidence-based practices in instruction. *US Department of Education.* Retrieved from https://ccrs.osepideasthatwork.org/teachers-academic/evidence-based-practices-instruction.

Klein, A. (2016). The Every Student Succeeds Act: An ESSA overview. Retrieved from http://www.edweek.org/ew/issues/every-student-succeeds-act/index.html.

Kretlow, A., and Helf, S. (2013). Teacher implementation of evidence-based practices in Tier 1: A national survey. *Teacher Education and Special Education,* 36(3), 167–85. https://doi.org/10.1177/0888406413489838.

Maheady, L., Rafferty, L., Patti, A., and Budin, S. (2016). Leveraging change: Influencing the implementation of evidence-based practice to improve outcomes for students with disabilities. *Learning Disabilities: A Contemporary Journal,* 14(2), 109–20. Retrieved from http://www.ldw-ldcj.org/index.php/open-access-articles/8-testblog/61-leveraging-evidence-based-practices-from-policy-to-action.html.

Mason-Williams, L., Frederick, J. R., and Mulcahy, C. A. (2015). Building adaptive expertise and practice-based evidence: Applying the implementation stages framework to special education teacher preparation. *Teacher Education and Special Education,* 38(3), 207–20. https://doi.org/10.1177/0888406414551285.

Meyer, A., Rose, D., and Gordon, D. (2014). *Universal design for learning: Theory and practice.* Wakefield, MA: CAST.

Ministry of Education and British Columbia School Superintendent's Association. (2011). *Supporting students with learning disabilities: A guide for teachers.* Retrieved from http://www.bced.gov.bc.ca/specialed/docs/learning_disabilities_guide.pdf.

National Center on Universal Design for Learning. (2017). *UDL guidelines: Theory and practice.* Retrieved from http://www.udlcenter.org/aboutudl/udlguidelines_theorypractice.

Obiakor, F., Harris, M., Mutua, K., Rotatori, A., and Algozzine, B. (2012). Making inclusion work in general education classrooms. *Education and Treatment of Children,* 35, 477–90. Retrieved from https://www.thefreelibrary.com/Making+inclusion+work+in+general+education+classrooms.-a0301649979.

Sailor, W., and Roger, B. (2005). Rethinking inclusion: Schoolwide applications. *Phi Delta Kappan,* 86, 503–9. https://doi.org/10.1177/003172170508600707.

Scheeler, M., Budin, S., and Markelz, A. (2016). The role of teacher preparation in evidence-based practices in schools. *Learning Disabilities: A Contemporary Journal,* 14(2), 171–87. Retrieved from http://www.ldw-ldcj.org/index.php/open-access-articles/8-testblog/64-the-role-of-teacher-preparation-in-promoting-evidence-based-practice-in-schools.html.

Scruggs, T., Mastropieri, M., and Marshak, L. (2012). Peer-mediated instruction in inclusive secondary social studies learning: Direct and indirect learning effects. *Learning Disabilities Research and Practice,* 27, 12–20. https://doi.org/10.1111/j.1540-5826.2011.00346.

Skrtic, T., Harris, K., and Shriner, J. (2005). The context of special education practice today. In T. Skrtic, K. Harris, and J. Shriner (eds), *Special education policy and practice: Accountability, instruction, and social changes* (pp. 1–28). Denver, CO: Love.

Solis, M., Vaughn, S., Swanson, E., and McCulley, L. (2012). Collaborative models of instruction: The empirical foundation of inclusion and co-teaching. *Psychology in the Schools,* 49, 498–510. Retrieved from https://eric.ed.gov/?id=EJ989971.

Tomlinson, C. (2014). *The differentiated classroom: Responding to the needs of all learners.* 2nd ed. Alexandria, VA: ASCD.

US Department of Education. (2004). *Individuals with Disabilities Education Improvement Act.* Retrieved from: http://idea.ed.gov/explore/home.html.

US Department of Education, Institute of Education Sciences, National Center for Education Evaluation and Regional Assistance. (2003). Identifying and implementing educational practices supported by rigorous evidence: A user-friendly guide. *Coalition for Evidence-Based Policy*. Retrieved from https://www2.ed.gov/rschstat/research/pubs/rigorousevid/rigorousevid.pdf.

Wiggins, G., and McTighe, J. (2005). *Understanding by design*. 2nd ed. Alexandria, VA: ASCD.

Chapter Four

Memory-Enhancing Strategies for Students with Learning Disabilities

Lessons Learned from Thirty-Five Years of Experimental Research

Margo A. Mastropieri, Thomas E. Scruggs, Anya Evmenova, and Kelley Regan, *George Mason University*

Problems with semantic memory are among the most commonly reported characteristics of learning disabilities, impacting virtually every academic area. For the past thirty-five years, the authors of this chapter have studied the effects of mnemonic (memory-enhancing) instruction on the learning and memory of students with learning disabilities. These investigations have evolved from basic research paradigms to applied practice, including individually administered laboratory-type experiments, small group investigations, whole-class applications, and applied teacher research.

Among the more commonly described characteristics of students with learning disabilities are deficits in areas related to memory. Research over the years has identified relative deficits in such areas as short-term memory, long-term memory, memory search, memory span, spontaneous use of strategies such as rehearsal and clustering, semantic memory, and working memory (Swanson, Cooney, and McNamara, 2004). The implications of such research are clear from examination of the ways these deficits can manifest in classroom situations.

The authors of this chapter had each accumulated a very substantial amount of anecdotal evidence from classroom and clinical settings that indicated students with learning disabilities, on elementary and secondary levels, commonly forgot information they had acquired only recently. Among the forgotten information were: things to do on a given day, such as completing (and returning) homework, asking for clarification of a previous assignment, locker combinations, classroom assignments, and bringing relevant books and materials to class.

In addition, it was often noted that students with learning disabilities had forgotten academic content that they had studied and discussed relatively previously. Most of this information had been verbally encoded in some fashion, yet was often completely gone when the time came to retrieve it (e.g., on tests). This deficit, in semantic (verbally based) memory, could be a particular problem.

Students in schools are required to learn and remember an enormous volume of verbal information relevant to the world around us. Although comprehension, elaboration, and reasoning are very much valued by schools, classroom tests commonly require students to retrieve sets of this vast store of verbal content. In order to be successful in school, students must be able to answer higher-order questions such as:

- What countries were associated with the Central Powers in World War I?
- What is the hardness level of rhodochrosite according to the Mohs scale?
- What is the meaning of "hirsute"?
- What are the five classes of vertebrates?
- What is the definition of radial symmetry in invertebrate animals? Provide examples.
- What was the Zimmerman note?
- What is the capital of Wyoming?
- What elements make up the halogens on the periodic table?

Although students are also expected to describe, discuss, organize, evaluate, compare, expand, or elaborate upon such information, their ability to accomplish this is typically predicated upon their ability to remember the information in the first place. Unfortunately, this ability is often lacking in students with learning disabilities (Swanson et al., 2004).

LABORATORY RESEARCH ON MNEMONIC STRATEGIES

Beginning in the early 1980s, the authors of this chapter began experimenting with mnemonic (memory-enhancing) techniques to increase the amount of information students with learning disabilities could remember, and to extend the amount of time they could retain this information. Some mnemonic instructional research had been conducted previously on normally achieving students (Pressley, Levin, and Delaney, 1982); however, at that time it was not known whether students with learning disabilities could meet the information-processing demands inherent in the strategies.

The Keyword Method

Because early research questions addressed whether different types and configurations of mnemonic strategies could be used effectively at all—that is, under any set of circumstances—true experimental designs were first employed with random assignment of individual students to experimental condition and one-to-one instruction. In this way, it was reasoned that the issue of potential efficacy could be addressed. If results from this research were successful, then questions addressing more realistic classroom applications could be addressed.

For example, an early study addressed whether students with learning disabilities could benefit from the keyword method in their learning and recall of vocabulary words (Mastropieri, Scruggs, Levin, Gaffney, and McLoone, 1985). Thirty-two junior-high students (twenty-one boys, eleven girls) with learning disabilities, with mean age of thirteen years, eleven months, were assigned at random to experimental and control conditions, after stratifying for grade level, and taught fourteen low-frequency vocabulary words taken from a Scrabble dictionary. These words (e.g., bugsha, ranid, dorado, dogbane, carline) were selected because they were suitable for the keyword method and because they were very unlikely to be known by students.

In both conditions, students were taught two practice words to become familiar with the procedures for each condition. Then the target words were taught. In the control ("direct instruction") condition, the experimenter first practiced all new vocabulary words to familiarize the student. Then the definitions for the words were taught using drill and practice. For example, the experimenter would say, "Bugsha means money. What does bugsha mean? Good. Bugsha means money."

The experimenter would then go to the next word. Words were practiced in sets of five, five, and four, whereby the set would be practiced, then reviewed, before moving to the next set. Cumulative reviews were provided. While the words were being practiced, the experimenter displayed a card containing the word, the definition, and a picture of the word. In the case of "bugsha," the card provided the word and definition on the top, and a picture of a stack of money in the middle. In the experimental (keyword) condition, students were first taught the keywords for each vocabulary word. A keyword is a word that sounds like the new word but can be easily pictured.

For example, a good keyword for bugsha is "bug," since it sounds like the first part of bugsha and can be pictured. After the keywords were learned, the experimenter displayed a card with a mnemonic picture for each word, linking the keyword with the definition. For example, for bugsha, the card provided the vocabulary word, keyword and meaning on the top, and a picture of a bug crawling on a stack of money in the center (the experimental and control pictures were identical except for the bug). When instructional time had expired (time in learning was the same for each condition), students were asked the definition of each word.

Analysis of results revealed that the mean differences by condition were not merely statistically significant but that students in the mnemonic keyword condition outperformed students in the control condition by a very wide margin of 79.5 percent correct vs. 31.2 percent correct. These results suggested that not only could students with learning disabilities benefit from using the keyword method but also that they could benefit very substantially. In a second experiment with a different sample of junior high students with learning disabilities, it was observed that mnemonic condition students learned more than controls, even when they constructed their own interactive images.

Additional experiments were conducted on vocabulary learning, using similar methodology, to replicate the findings, and to address some additional research questions. Using a crossover design, it was discovered that students with mental retardation could also benefit from the keyword method for learning vocabulary, performing far better (71.5 percent correct) than a drill-and-practice rehearsal condition (48.0 percent correct) (Scruggs, Mastropieri, and Levin, 1985).

Another finding showed that junior high school students with learning disabilities were able to learn foreign language vocabulary using the keyword method, and could create substantial components of the strategy themselves, greatly outperforming control conditions when doing so (Scruggs, Mastropieri, McLoone, and Levin, 1987). Additionally, an experiment by Mastropieri, Scruggs, and Fulk (1990) provided evidence that students with learning disabilities could use mnemonic strategies to learn abstract ("saprophytic") vocabulary as well as concrete ("catafalque") vocabulary, and perform far better than control conditions on recall tests as well as tests of comprehension.

States and capitals were taught in a keyword-keyword strategy in a counterbalanced design across two self-contained classrooms. For example, to learn that Annapolis is the capital of Maryland, a picture of a couple eating apples (keyword for Annapolis) was shown while getting married (keyword for Maryland). In this investigation, students learned far more under mnemonic instruction, whether they were asked for the state or for the capital. Teachers and students alike expressed preference for the keyword method.

Evidence of the facilitative effects of the keyword method for students with learning disabilities was also provided by Condus, Marshall, and Miller (1986), who reported superior long-term retention over a ten-week period by mnemonically instructed twelve-year-old students. Confirmation of the facilitative vocabulary-learning effects of the keyword method was also provided by Berry (1986), in two experiments with fourth- and fifth-grade students with learning disabilities as well as normally achieving students.

In a related set of investigations, Brigham, Scruggs, and Mastropieri (1995), and Scruggs, Mastropieri, Brigham, and Sullivan (1992) used the keyword method to teach students the locations of important battles in American history. In the Scruggs et al. (1992) investigation, students with learning disabilities were better able to identify the location of the battle (taught using a map marked, for example, with a tiger for Fort Ticonderoga rather than a representative illustration), and better to recall the winner of the battle (coded blue for American vs. red for British in both conditions).

In a second investigation, Brigham et al. (1995) found that students could also better recall related information encoded with the keyword (e.g., the tiger firing a cannon to promote recall that cannon taken at Fort Ticonderoga were captured and moved to Boston). These investigations further underlined the versatility of the keyword method and provided information that performance even on a spatial learning task can be to a great extent mediated by language-based elaborations.

The Pegword Method

Other research questions addressed the versatility of mnemonic strategies to help students encode and retain other types of content. Mastropieri, Scruggs, and Levin (1985a) investigated whether students with learning disabilities could benefit from a strategy that employed both mnemonic keywords and mnemonic pegwords for remembering numbered or ordered information. In this case, we used these mnemonic strategies for teaching the hardness levels of North American minerals, using the Mohs scale, which provides a hardness ranking of all minerals. For example, the mineral wolframite is typically hardness level 4, on a scale from 1 (talc) to 10 (diamond).

In this experiment, ninth-grade students with learning disabilities (mean age fourteen years, nine months) were divided into relatively low vs. relatively high reading comprehenders, and individually assigned at random to one of three conditions: mnemonic, direct instruction, and free study. All students individually were taught the hardness levels of fourteen North American minerals—for example, gypsum = hardness level 2; calcite = hardness level 3; quartz = hardness level 7; apatite = hardness level 8.

For all conditions, students first were prefamiliarized with their respective experimental condition. Then students were taught target content according to the condition. In the free study condition, students were provided with pictures, printed lists of minerals and hardness levels, flash cards, and paper and pencil, and told to use their own best method for studying. In the direct instruction condition, experimenters provided direct drill and practice on the minerals and hardness levels ("Wolframite is hardness level 4. What hardness level is wolframite? Good, wolframite is hardness level 4.") During drill and practice, students were shown cards on which were printed color pictures of minerals, with their name and hardness level printed above the picture.

In the mnemonic condition, students were taught the keywords for each of the minerals (e.g., wolframite = wolf), and the pegwords for the numbers 1 to 10 (e.g., one is bun, two is shoe, three is tree, four is door). Students were then shown a mnemonic picture and given practice learning and applying the strategy. For example, for wolframite, students were shown a card containing the mineral, keyword, and hardness level printed on top, and in the center an illustration of a wolf standing at a door.

Students were asked the hardness level for each of the fourteen minerals after instruction; after a twenty-four-hour delay interval, students were given a surprise recall test of the mineral hardness levels. Mnemonically instructed students remembered 75.2 percent of the minerals presented on the immediate test, and, surprisingly, remembered even more (78.1 percent) after a twenty-four-hour delay interval. In sharp contrast, free study condition students recalled only 36.5 percent on the immediate test and had forgotten all but 27.8 percent on the delayed test. Finally, students in the direct instruction condition remembered only 25.5 percent for the test of immediate recall, and remembered even less (21.9 percent) on the delayed test.

The fact that students recalled more in the free study condition than in the drill-and-practice condition was surprising, and suggested that students with learning disabilities may be able to some extent to utilize study strategies that are somewhat superior to simple rehearsal. The differences, however, were not great, and both comparison conditions performed far below the mnemonic condition. Finally, a condition x comprehension ability interaction revealed that higher comprehenders scored differentially higher in the free study condition.

In a replication of this study, Mastropieri, Scruggs, and Levin (1986) taught hardness levels of North American minerals to junior high school students with learning disabilities, in small groups of students that had been randomly assigned to condition. Differences again favored the mnemonic condition, suggesting that mnemonic strategies could be taught to students in small groups.

In a second experiment, students with mental retardation benefited from the keyword-pegword strategy over drill and practice, although we found that the pegwords had to be pretrained, and took a surprisingly long time to learn. Finally, one investigation concluded that students could use multiple representations of a single pegword (e.g., hornblende, apatite, and actinolite are all hardness level 5) without confusion (Scruggs, Mastropieri, and Levin, 1986).

In a later application of Mastropieri, Scruggs, Bakken, Brigham, and Whedon's (1997) keyword-pegword method, students with learning disabilities (mean age fourteen years, three months) were taught the orders of US presidents over a six-week period. For example, to teach that Pierce was the fourteenth president, students were presented with a picture of someone forking (sticking a fork in) a purse.

In this case, forking was a pegword for fourteen, and purse was a keyword for Pierce. In a comparison condition, students were taught using pictures of the president and the number of the president. Two weeks following the six weeks of instruction, results indicated that mnemonically instructed content was far better remembered than traditionally instructed content, even though the mnemonic content was presented in the first three weeks, or five to eight weeks prior to the test.

As a further extension of this keyword-pegword method (Scruggs, Mastropieri, Levin, and Gaffney, 1985), mnemonic pictures were used to teach students not just the hardness levels of minerals but also a common color and a common use of each mineral. Thus, it was taught not just that wolframite has a hardness level 4 but also that it is black in color and used for making light bulbs (from tungsten ore for the filaments).

Junior high school students with learning disabilities were randomly assigned to one of four conditions: free study, direct instruction, reduced-list direct instruction (in which only half the content was taught in the same amount of time), and mnemonic. Students in each condition received initial practice on the procedures and materials in their respective condition. Free students were provided with a variety of materials and told to use their own best method for studying.

Students in the direct instruction conditions received direct drill and practice on the minerals and their attributes. Students were shown cards that contained pictures of the minerals and verbal presentation of the minerals' hardness, color, and use. The full-list condition received drill and practice on three attributes each of eight minerals (or twenty-four total facts), while the reduced-list condition received drill and practice on three attributes each of four minerals (or twelve total facts).

In the mnemonic condition, students were shown cards containing the mineral name, keyword, hardness level, pegword, and listing of color and use. The picture depicted the keyword with the color of the mineral interacting with the pegword representation and use. For example, for the mineral wolframite, students were shown an illustration of a black (color) wolf (keyword for wolframite) standing at a door (pegword for four) lit by light bulbs (common use).

Results of this investigation revealed that students taught mnemonically dramatically outperformed students taught in every other condition. Students taught in the reduced-list (four minerals) direct instruction condition remembered no higher of a percentage of information than students taught mnemonically (eight minerals). Again, free study students performed descriptively higher than direct instruction condition students, suggesting that direct drill and practice may be no better strategy for this type of content than students studying independently in a structured, supervised condition.

After this investigation, a number of experimental mineral attribute studies were conducted, including dichotomized facts about minerals (e.g., hard vs. soft; industrial vs. domestic use; light vs. dark) (Scruggs, Mastropieri, McLoone, and Levin, 1987), and mnemonic information about minerals embedded in text (Scruggs, Mastropieri, McLoone, and Levin, 1987). In two randomized experiments, it was determined that students with learning disabilities using mnemonic strategies greatly outperformed students who studied mineral attributes using visual-spatial illustrations to organize content. This was true whether the minerals were represented as continuous or as dichotomized facts.

In this investigation, students in the visual-spatial condition did not outperform students in a free study condition (Scruggs, Mastropieri, Levin, McLoone, Gaffney, and Prater, 1985). Overall, it was concluded that students with learning disabilities could profit greatly from a variety of mnemonic representations and, in fact, performed greatly beyond the learning and memory of content achieved through experimenter-directed rehearsal, visual-spatial display, or free study procedures. The reasons for this are not entirely known and cannot be derived directly from the results of these experiments.

It is known, however, that mnemonic strategies interact favorably with areas of relative strength for students with learning disabilities (e.g., memory for pictures, ability to retrieve information from acoustic cues, provided elaborations) and de-emphasize areas of relative weakness (reading, memory store, spontaneous verbal elaboration). For these reasons, it is thought mnemonic strategies are particularly effective for students with learning disabilities (Mastropieri, Scruggs, and Levin, 1985b).

CLASSROOM APPLICATIONS

Although there was substantial evidence of the potential efficacy of mnemonic strategies, they had not been tested over time in classroom-like situations. The researchers were unsure if such strategies could be applied to multiple lessons in a unit of instruction, or whether the advantage students realized after a single lesson might begin to deteriorate with multiple mnemonic presentations.

It was known from previous research that students were more likely to become confused in comparison conditions; we did not know whether mnemonic instruction over consecutive days would lead to confusion. Therefore, a series of investigations was planned to study applications of mnemonic strategies.

Multiple Lessons

Veit, Scruggs, and Mastropieri (1986) developed materials to teach three lessons about dinosaurs to middle school students with learning disabilities, over a period of three days. Students were taught in small groups (two to four students), and twenty-four groups were randomly assigned to mnemonic and comparison conditions. Lessons were provided in counterbalanced order, so that learning and memory over time could be evaluated separately from relative lesson difficulty. In one lesson, students were taught, via experimenter-led drill and practice or mnemonic strategies, root words for fourteen dinosaur names (e.g., ptero-, meaning "winged"; saur, meaning "lizard").

Students were tested on their recall of the root words and were also given an unpracticed test of combined root words (e.g., What does pterosaur mean?). In another lesson, students were taught attributes of eight dinosaurs, including herbivore or carnivore, period of existence, and a specific attribute. For example, brachiosaurus lived in the middle (Jurassic) period, was a plant-eater, and was the biggest dinosaur known at that time. In a third lesson, students were taught a number of reasons offered for dinosaur extinction, in order of plausibility (e.g., reason #3: an exploding star killed the dinosaurs).

In the dinosaur names lesson, students in the mnemonic condition were taught using the keyword method (e.g., for ptero-, a picture of a tire with wings), while comparison condition students received drill and practice. For the dinosaur attributes lesson, students in the mnemonic condition were taught using the same procedures as the mineral attributes lesson.

For example, the keyword for brachiosaurus was given as "broccoli," and a picture was provided of a giant green (plant-eater) broccoli in a midday scene (middle or Jurassic period), with someone saying, "That's the biggest broccoli ever!" (biggest dinosaur). In the comparison condition, students were provided drill and practice and shown all relevant information on a visual-spatial display, which portrayed period, type of diet, and specific attribute in a spatially organized illustration.

For the extinction lessons, comparison condition students received descriptive pictures and drill and practice. Mnemonic condition students received pictures containing pegwords for each ordered reason. For example, for reason #3 (an exploding star killed the dinosaurs), students were shown a picture of a dinosaur in front of a Christmas tree, on the top of which was a star, exploding.

After each day of instruction, students were given a test of the lesson's content. Twenty-four hours after the third lesson, students were given a cumulative unit test. Results indicated that students in the mnemonic condition significantly (and substantially) outperformed students in the comparison condition, for each of the three lessons as well as for the cumulative test. Mnemonic condition students also performed better on a test of application of dinosaur root words.

Examination of test scores by day of instruction revealed that performance in either condition neither increased nor decreased over the three days. In addition, examination of intralist intrusions (incorrect answers from within the same set of answers) revealed that confusion was more likely in the comparison condition than in the mnemonic condition. Overall, it was considered that mnemonic instruction could be effective in longer-term classroom applications.

The list of reasons for dinosaur extinction was also employed in a study of prose learning of students with learning disabilities (Mastropieri, Scruggs, and Levin, 1987). In this investigation, students who were shown pegwords outperformed students who were shown descriptive pictures and students in a free study condition; however, students in neither picture condition remembered more related information that was also pictured (e.g., dinosaurs died out from disease more easily because all continents were connected).

Reconstructive Elaborations

The next study looked at how mnemonic instruction might be adapted to existing school curriculum, over longer periods of time. In an initial examination of school content, it was determined that all relevant content could not be easily encoded into keyword and pegword representations and that associative content needed to be considered with respect to its concreteness and meaningfulness. That is, information that is already concrete and meaningful (e.g., trenches in World War I were unhealthy) may need simply to be presented in a representative (mimetic) picture, such as a picture of sick soldiers in trenches.

Information that is meaningful but abstract (e.g., US foreign policy) may be presented in a symbolic representation (e.g., Uncle Sam). Thus, US policy of neutrality at the beginning of World War I could be represented by Uncle Sam declining to support either side. Information that is neither familiar nor meaningful (such as unknown proper names, such as the Zimmerman telegram) can be presented in an acoustic representation, such as a keyword.

For information that includes a series or list (such as the countries in the Allied Powers), letter strategies, including acronyms or acrostics, may be appropriate. This technique of analyzing content to create memory-enhancing strategies we referred to as reconstructive elaborations (Mastropieri and Scruggs, 1989c).

The researchers (Scruggs and Mastropieri, 1989b) used this model of reconstructing content to mimetic, symbolic, and acoustic representations to develop curriculum relevant to the study of World War I. We then taught this content in a single lesson to thirty junior high and high school students classified as having learning disabilities ($n = 28$) or mild mental retardation ($n = 2$), with a mean age of 15.1, and an average reading level of fifth grade. Individual students were assigned at random to mnemonic and comparison conditions, and were taught the content individually by trained experimenters.

Experimenters read passages of text and demonstrated mnemonic pictures and techniques where indicated. Students in the comparison condition were read the same text and referred to descriptive pictures of the same content. Analysis of results indicated that students in the reconstructive elaborations condition learned nearly twice as much information as comparison condition students and maintained this advantage over a delayed recall interval.

After the success of this investigation, Scruggs and Mastropieri (1989a) adapted curriculum in US history to the model of reconstructive elaborations, and applied it to four special education classrooms for an eight-week unit covering World War I, the 1920s, the 1930s, and World War II. Using a crossover design, each class received mnemonic and comparison condition (representative pictures) instruction in a counterbalanced order, alternated every two weeks, so that one class received instruction in order mnemonic-comparison-mnemonic-comparison, and another class received instruction in the opposite order.

A third class received three units of instruction in the mnemonic condition over six weeks, followed by one unit of instruction in the comparison condition over two weeks, while a fourth class received instruction in the opposite order.

Students were tested after every two-week chapter, and after eight weeks of instruction, students received a cumulative unit examination. Again, students when instructed mnemonically performed much higher than when instructed by more traditional means, with average scores of 75.6 percent vs. 44.0 percent correct, respectively. This study was replicated in another eight-week implementation with a sample of seventh and eighth graders with learning disabilities who not only received higher test scores but also higher grades when instructed mnemonically (Scruggs and Mastropieri, 1989a).

In a similar investigation using a crossover design (Mastropieri and Scruggs, 1989b), students with learning disabilities when taught mnemonically outperformed traditional instruction performances in the study of state (Indiana) history, in both immediate and one-week delayed recall (see also

Fontana, Mastropieri, and Scruggs, 2007, for a description of a high school social studies classroom implementation using mnemonics).

In another classroom application, middle school students with learning disabilities in two self-contained classes were taught science content via mnemonic or traditional instruction in a crossover design in which each class alternated treatments for the first two weeks. The method of reconstructive elaborations was again employed, using mimetic pictures for familiar information (the earthworm is a roundworm with a segmented body and many hearts), symbolic pictures (e.g., a warm sunny day representing warm-blooded animals), and acoustic keywords (e.g., pear for parasite; radio cemetery for radial symmetry).

The examiners also employed letter strategies (FARM-B) for representing the five classes of vertebrates (fish, amphibian, reptile, mammal, bird). Again, students learned far more when instructed mnemonically (78.9 percent correct) than when instructed by traditional means (38.8 percent correct).

During a third week of instruction, all students were presented with mnemonic strategies for remembering information involving earth science. Students remembered 76.3 percent of information tested overall and answered correctly 93.7 percent of questions for which they reported using the appropriate mnemonic strategy.

During the fourth week, students were prompted and encouraged to create their own mnemonic strategies. Students were able to create their own strategies, and were generally successful when they did so and reported using the strategy; however, students overall scored only 52.5 percent correct on the unit, and learned only about one-third as much content as when they were provided with the strategies.

It was concluded that, overall, teachers needed to determine whether learning strategy use or learning academic content was more important when planning instruction. Other research has demonstrated that students with learning disabilities are capable of creating their own mnemonic strategies (Fulk, Mastropieri, and Scruggs, 1992; King-Sears, Mercer, and Sindelar, 1992).

Mnemonic strategies are more effectively and efficiently created and delivered by teachers; thus, it seems that optimally teachers would use mnemonic strategies in their own instruction, and at the same time, teach students to create their own strategies for other situations when mnemonic materials are not available.

APPLICATIONS IN INCLUSIVE CLASSES

Applications of mnemonic strategies may be extended in inclusive classes, and teacher applications of mnemonic strategies can be embedded within a model of differentiated instruction involving peer tutoring (Mastropieri and Scruggs, 2017; Regan, Evmenova, Mastropieri, and Scruggs, 2015). For example, students can proceed at different rates through the curriculum with peer tutoring using mnemonics in inclusive classes. In addition, materials can be designed to include mnemonic and other strategies to be used or not used depending on the students' needs. In addition, we studied the effects on student learning when teachers created and implemented their mnemonic materials.

Peer Tutoring

In one investigation, Mastropieri, Scruggs, and Graetz (2005) adapted materials for classwide peer tutoring in inclusive high school chemistry classes, fifteen of whom had disabilities. In this case, the mnemonic strategies were created by clip art rather than by artist's drawings. Students in the mnemonic condition worked with partners to study important class content, including endothermic and exothermic reactions, core and valence electrons, halogens, noble gases, periodic table of elements, and molarity.

Students questioned each other on key concepts, such as moles, the atomic weight in grams of an element or compound. If the student was unable to answer correctly, the tutor showed the tutee the appropriate strategy, in this case a picture of a mole (keyword for mole) sitting on a scale measuring its weight in grams. If the student answered correctly, the strategy was skipped. In each case, the tutor then asked the student to elaborate on the response, for example, "What else is important about moles?" and "What is an example of a mole?" In this way, verbal elaboration and comprehension-enhancing strategies were included with mnemonic strategies.

After several weeks of instruction, students were provided with a unit test, which revealed that mnemonically instructed students outperformed students taught more traditionally. Normally achieving students taught with peer-mediated mnemonic strategies outperformed comparison students by 14 percent; however, the advantage for students with learning disabilities was 43 percent.

Marshak, Mastropieri, and Scruggs (2011) designed tutoring materials that included directions for tutors to only provide the mnemonic strategy when needed by the tutee. In other words, materials included the strategy but the strategy was not used when students could learn the information using their memory or own strategies. Findings again revealed that students taught with the mnemonic materials recalled significantly more content than their control condition counterparts. In addition, teachers and students indicated they enjoyed using these mnemonic tutoring materials.

Teacher-Created Mnemonic Strategies

The chapter authors also examined how teachers use mnemonic strategies in their own classroom for particular curriculum demands. Terrill, Scruggs, and Mastropieri (2004) studied the effects of teacher-created and -implemented keyword mnemonic strategies for teaching SAT vocabulary to a group of high school students with learning disabilities. For example, to teach that the word "martinet" means "a strict disciplinarian," the teacher created a picture of a Martian (keyword for martinet) acting as a strict disciplinarian. Alternating mnemonic and traditional workbook treatments over a period of six weeks, Terrell et al. reported that students correctly recalled the meanings of 91.7 percent of words learned in the mnemonic condition but only 48.8 percent of the words learned in the traditional instruction condition.

Uberti, Scruggs, and Mastropieri (2003) described the effects of teacher-created mnemonic strategies for learning vocabulary from a book that was being read to three inclusive third-grade classes. In one class, teachers provided words and their definitions (e.g., jettison = throw overboard). In a second class, they provided the same words and definitions, and also illustrations (e.g., a jet throwing something overboard). In the third class, they were provided with keywords (e.g., jettison = jet) and shown an interactive picture (e.g., a jet throwing something overboard). In the "jettison" example, the only difference was an overt reference to "jet" as a keyword for "jettison."

Results indicated that both normally achieving students and students with learning disabilities benefited more greatly from the keyword condition, but that the students with learning disabilities benefited more greatly, remembering over three times more words than in the picture condition, while the mnemonic advantage of the normally achieving students was less pronounced.

Such differential facilitation of mnemonic strategies was also observed in a study by Mastropieri, Sweda, and Scruggs (2000), where the teacher constructed and implemented mnemonic strategies for teaching social studies content in inclusive classes. Although all student types benefited, students with learning disabilities benefited more from the strategies.

These investigations, taken with the findings of the Mastropieri, Scruggs, and Graetz (2005) investigation, suggest that mnemonic strategies may in fact narrow the performance gap between students with learning disabilities and normally achieving students. On the other hand, the fact that the effects may be less pronounced for normally achieving students may provide teachers with less motivation to include them in their instruction.

FINAL THOUGHTS

In more than three decades of research, a considerable amount has been learned about the efficacy and versatility of mnemonic strategies for students with learning disabilities. First of all, the power and consistency of these strategies in a variety of applications with students with learning disabilities is impressive. In quantitative research syntheses (Mastropieri and Scruggs, 1989a; Scruggs and Mastropieri, 2000), it was reported that mnemonic strategy instruction for students with mild disabilities was associated with effect sizes in excess of 1.5 standard deviations over a variety of comparison conditions, an extremely high value that places mnemonic instruction among the most efficacious treatments for students with learning disabilities.

These interventions are successful across content areas, grade levels, and type of implementation, including laboratory studies, classroom implementations, and educator applications. Teachers, therefore, can use mnemonic strategies with students with learning disabilities whenever difficulties in semantic memory for academic content are encountered with an assurance that they will provide positive outcomes (for a number of examples and applications, see Mastropieri and Scruggs, 2017).

From the early years of special education to the present day, there has been an explosion of effective strategies for promoting school success of students with learning disabilities, including self-management and self-monitoring, peer-assisted learning, phonemic awareness training, direct instruction, comprehension monitoring strategies, mathematics strategies, hands-on learning, study skills, and strategies for enhancing written language (Mastropieri and Scruggs, 2017). Mnemonic strategies, taken in this context, can provide an important element of an overall highly effective program of instruction for students with learning disabilities.

POINTS TO REMEMBER

- *Mnemonic strategies do not address all learning objectives, but when remembering academic information is required, mnemonic strategies are extremely powerful.*
- *Mnemonic strategies work best when they are carefully constructed using keywords that are familiar to students, and clearly picture interactions between the keyword or pegword and the to-be-associated information.*
- *As effective as mnemonic strategies are, they must be explained, practiced, and reviewed over time to maximize their potential for enhancing memory.*
- *Mnemonic strategies have been seen to enhance comprehension as well as memory. However, this is probably true only because mnemonically in-*

structed students have acquired more information that they can apply to comprehension tests. Teachers should be sure to match instructional strategies to instructional objectives when planning instruction, and be certain that comprehension objectives are also being met.
- One relative shortcoming of mnemonic strategies is that they can be time consuming to create. In the past, we have recommended brainstorming, especially with a partner, to help identify relevant keywords. To create mnemonic pictures, clip art can be extremely useful in creating suitable mnemonic pictures. A quick internet search will bring up literally hundreds of thousands of pictures. Once mnemonic strategies have been created, they can be used over and over again, to the great benefit of students with memory problems.

The primary author can be reached at mmastrop@gmu.edu.

REFERENCES

Berry, J. K. (1986). *Learning disabled children's use of mnemonic strategies for vocabulary learning (memory).* PhD diss,, University of Wisconsin, Madison.

Brigham, F. J., Scruggs, T. E., and Mastropieri, M. A. (1995). Elaborative maps for enhanced learning of historical information. *Journal of Special Education,* 28, 440–60. https://doi.org/10.1177/002246699502800404.

Condus, M. M., Marshall, K. J., and Miller, S. R. (1986). Effects of the keyword mnemonic strategy vocabulary acquisition and maintenance by learning disabled children. *Journal of Learning Disabilities,* 19, 609–13. https://doi.org/10.1177/002221948601901006.

Fontana, J., Mastropieri, M. A., and Scruggs, T. E. (2007). Mnemonic strategy instruction in inclusive secondary social studies classes. *Remedial and Special Education,* 28, 345–55. https://doi.org/10.1177/07419325070280060401.

Fulk, B. J. M., Mastropieri, M. A., and Scruggs, T. E. (1992). Mnemonic generalization training with learning disabled adolescents. *Learning Disabilities Research and Practice,* 7, 2–10. https://doi.org/10.2307/1510353.

King-Sears, M. E., Mercer, C. D., and Sindelar, P. T. (1992). Toward independence with keyword mnemonics: A strategy for science vocabulary instruction. *Remedial and Special Education,* 13(5), 22–33. https://doi.org/10.1177/074193259201300505.

Marshak, L., Mastropieri, M. A., and Scruggs, T. E. (2011). Curriculum enhancements for inclusive secondary social studies classes. *Exceptionality,* 19(2), 61–74. Retrieved from https://eric.ed.gov/?id=EJ923893.

Mastropieri, M. A., and Scruggs, T. E. (1988). Increasing the content area learning of learning disabled students: Research implementation. *Learning Disabilities Research,* 4, 17–25. Retrieved from https://eric.ed.gov/?id=EJ393662.

———. (1989a). Constructing more meaningful relationships: Mnemonic instruction for special populations. *Educational Psychology Review,* 1, 83–111. https://doi.org/10.1007/BF01326638.

———. (1989b). Mnemonic social studies instruction: Classroom applications. *Remedial and Special Education,* 10(3), 40–46. https://doi.org/10.1177/074193258901000308.

———. (1989c). Reconstructive elaborations: Strategies that facilitate content learning. *Learning Disabilities Focus,* 4, 73–77. https://doi.org/10.3102/00028312026002311.

———. (1991). *Teaching students ways to remember: Strategies for learning mnemonically.* Cambridge, MA: Brookline Books.

———. (2017). *The inclusive classroom: Strategies for effective differentiated instruction.* 6th ed. Englewood Cliffs, NJ: Pearson Education.

Mastropieri, M. A., Scruggs, T. E., Bakken, J. P., and Brigham, F. J. (1992). A complex mnemonic strategy for teaching states and capitals: Comparing forward and backward associations. *Learning Disabilities Research and Practice*, 7, 96–103. Retrieved from https://eric.ed.gov/?id=EJ443023.

Mastropieri, M. A., Scruggs, T. E., Bakken, J. P., Brigham, F. J., and Whedon, C. (1997). Using mnemonic strategies to teach information about U.S. presidents: A classroom-based investigation. *Learning Disability Quarterly*, 20, 13–21. https://doi.org/10.2307/1511089.

Mastropieri, M. A., Scruggs, T. E., and Fulk, B. J. M. (1990). Teaching abstract vocabulary with the keyword method: Effects on recall and comprehension. *Journal of Learning Disabilities*, 23, 92–96. https://doi.org/10.1177/002221949002300203.

Mastropieri, M. A., Scruggs, T. E., and Graetz, J. (2005). Cognition and learning in inclusive high school chemistry classes. In T. E. Scruggs and M. A. Mastropieri (eds.), *Advances in learning and behavioral disabilities*. Vol. 18, *Cognition and learning in diverse settings* (pp. 107–18). Oxford, UK: Elsevier.

Mastropieri, M. A., Scruggs, T. E., and Levin, J. R. (1985a). Mnemonic strategy instruction with learning disabled adolescents. *Journal of Learning Disabilities*, 18, 94–100. https://doi.org/10.1177/002221948501800207.

———. (1985b). Maximizing what exceptional students can learn: A review of research on the keyword method and related mnemonic techniques. *Remedial and Special Education*, 6(2), 39–45. https://doi.org/10.1177/074193258500600208.

———. (1986). Direct vs. mnemonic instruction: Relative benefits for exceptional learners. *Journal of Special Education*, 20, 299–308. https://doi.org/10.1177/002246698602000304.

———. (1987). Learning disabled students' memory for expository prose: Mnemonic vs. nonmnemonic pictures. *American Educational Research Journal*, 24, 505–19. https://doi.org/10.3102/00028312024004505.

Mastropieri, M. A., Scruggs, T. E., Levin, J. R., Gaffney, J., and McLoone, B. (1985). Mnemonic vocabulary instruction for learning disabled students. *Learning Disability Quarterly*, 8, 57–63. https://doi.org/10.2307/1510908.

Mastropieri, M. A., Scruggs, T. E., and McLoone, B., Levin, J. R. (1987). Facilitating learning disabled students' acquisition of science classifications. *Learning Disability Quarterly*, 8, 299–309. https://doi.org/10.2307/1510593.

Mastropieri, M. A., Sweda, J., and Scruggs, T. E. (2000). Putting mnemonic strategies to work in an inclusive classroom. *Learning Disabilities Research and Practice*, 15, 69–74. Retrieved from https://eric.ed.gov/?id=EJ608054.

Pressley, M., Levin, J., and Delaney, H. D. (1982). The mnemonic keyword method. *Review of Educational Research*, 52, 61–91. https://doi.org/10.3102/00346543052001061.

Regan, K., Evmenova, A. S., Mastropieri, M. A., and Scruggs, T. E. (2015). Peer interactions in the content areas: Using differentiated instruction strategies. In K. R. Harris and L. Meltzer (eds.), *The power of peers in the classroom* (pp. 33–68). New York: Guilford.

Scruggs, T. E., and Mastropieri, M. A. (1989a). Mnemonic instruction of learning disabled students: A field-based evaluation. *Learning Disability Quarterly*, 12, 119–25. https://doi.org/10.2307/1510727.

———. (1989b). Reconstructive elaborations: A model for content area learning. *American Educational Research Journal*, 26, 311–27. https://doi.org/10.3102/00028312026002311.

———. (1992). Classroom applications of mnemonic instruction: Acquisition, maintenance, and generalization. *Exceptional Children*, 58, 219–29. https://doi.org/10.1177/001440299105800305.

———. (2000). The effectiveness of mnemonic instruction for students with learning and behavior problems: Research synthesis. *Journal of Behavioral Education*, 10, 163–73. https://doi.org/10.1023/A:1016640214368.

Scruggs, T. E., Mastropieri, M. A., Brigham, F. J., and Sullivan, G. S. (1992). Effects of mnemonic reconstructions on the spatial learning of adolescents with learning disabilities. *Learning Disability Quarterly*, 15, 154–62. https://doi.org/10.2307/1510240.

Scruggs, T. E., Mastropieri, M. A., and Levin, J. R. (1985). Vocabulary acquisition by mentally retarded students under direct and mnemonic instruction. *American Journal of Mental Deficiency*, 89, 546–51. Retrieved from https://www.ncbi.nlm.nih.gov/pubmed/3993698.

———. (1986). Can children effectively re-use the same mnemonic pegwords? *Educational Communication and Technology Journal,* 34, 83–88. https://doi.org/10.1007/BF02802580.

Scruggs, T. E., Mastropieri, M. A., Levin, J. R., and Gaffney, J. S. (1985). Facilitating the acquisition of science facts in learning disabled students. *American Educational Research Journal,* 22, 575–86. https://doi.org/10.3102/00028312022004575.

Scruggs, T. E., Mastropieri, M. A., Levin, J. R., McLoone, B. B., Gaffney, J. S., and Prater, M. (1985). Increasing content-area learning: A comparison of mnemonic and visual-spatial direct instruction. *Learning Disabilities Research,* 1, 18–31. Retrieved from https://eric.ed.gov/?id=EJ334325.

Scruggs, T. E., Mastropieri, M. A., McLoone, B. B., and Levin, J. R. (1987). Learning disabled students' memory for expository prose: Mnemonic versus nonmnemonic pictures. *Journal of Educational Psychology,* 79, 27–34. https://doi.org/10.3102/00028312024004505.

Swanson, H. L., Cooney, J. B., and McNamara, J. K. (2004). Learning disabilities and memory. In B. Y. L. Wong (ed.), *Learning about learning disabilities* (pp. 315–39). 3rd ed. San Diego, CA: Elsevier Academic Press.

Terrill, C., Scruggs, T. E., and Mastropieri, M. A. (2004). SAT vocabulary instruction for high school students with learning disabilities. *Intervention in School and Clinic,* 39, 288–94. https://doi.org/10.1177/10534512040390050501.

Uberti, H. Z., Scruggs, T. E., and Mastropieri, M. A. (2003). Keywords make the difference! Mnemonic instruction in inclusive classrooms. *Teaching Exceptional Children,* 35(3), 56–61. https://doi.org/10.1177/004005990303500308.

Veit, D. T., Scruggs, T. E., and Mastropieri, M. A. (1986). Extended mnemonic instruction with learning disabled students. *Journal of Educational Psychology,* 78, 300–308. Retrieved from https://eric.ed.gov/?id=ED267544.

Chapter Five

Mnemonic Strategies

What Are They, How Can I Use Them, and How Effective Are They?

Margo A. Mastropieri, Thomas E. Scruggs, Kelley Regan, Anya Evmenova, and Judith Fontana, *George Mason University*

Many students with learning disabilities experience difficulties when required to learn school-related information. The demands of learning and remembering vast amounts of new content in domains such as science, social studies, and vocabulary increase greatly as students advance in grade level. The importance associated with learning and remembering school information has also increased as school performance and graduation requirements have become linked to standards on statewide high-stakes tests. This has led to increased concern on the part of many students with learning disabilities; as expressed by one student: "How do they expect me to remember all this stuff?"

Many methods for enhancing memory have existed for years, some going back as far as the time of the Ancient Greeks (see Yates, 1956, for a discussion). One strategy that has proven particularly effective for helping students with learning disabilities to learn and remember unfamiliar school-related content is mnemonic strategy instruction (Forness, Kavale, Blum, and Lloyd, 1997).

Mnemonic (memory-enhancing) strategy instruction helps make unfamiliar information more concrete and familiar by linking new information with prior knowledge using visual and auditory cues. This enhanced familiarity and concreteness helps make information more memorable. The most effective mnemonic strategies use systematic encoding techniques and direct retrieval links to recently learned information (Mastropieri and Scruggs, 1998). In addition, mnemonic strategies that are especially effective utilize elaborations in which pieces of information are linked together in interactive images, pictures, or verbal phrases.

Although typically developing students may begin to use types of elaborative mnemonic strategies independently, students with learning disabilities frequently do not. Fortunately, however, research has demonstrated that when students with learning disabilities are taught using mnemonic strategies, their performance increases significantly (Mastropieri and Scruggs, 2018; Scruggs and Mastropieri, 2000).

WHAT ARE MNEMONIC STRATEGIES?

One example of a mnemonic strategy that provides encoding and retrieval features and interactive elaborations is the keyword method. The keyword method works best when newly introduced information is unfamiliar and needs to be linked to already familiar information. When using the keyword strategy, unfamiliar information is first made more concrete by changing the new and unfamiliar word into an acoustically similar but concrete word.

For example, to learn that the vocabulary word "buncombe" means "empty, insincere speech or talk," first, think of an acoustically similar, familiar, and easily pictured keyword. In this case, bun would be a good keyword because it sounds like buncombe, is concrete, and is easily pictured. Then, think of an interactive picture of a bun and its definition doing something together. In this example, a picture of a person giving an insincere or empty speech with the audience throwing buns at the speaker would be a good example.

When asked to retrieve the word *buncombe*, first, think of the acoustically similar, concrete, and familiar keyword *bun*. Then think back to what was happening in the picture with the bun in it; in this case, it was "an audience throwing buns at a speaker delivering an insincere and empty speech." Finally, retrieve "insincere speech or empty talk" as the definition of buncombe (Mastropieri, Scruggs, and Fulk, 1990). In this case, the definition can be enhanced with an audience member stating, "This speech is empty, insincere, and contrived!!"

Mnemonic strategies are versatile and can be used in many different ways to facilitate learning unfamiliar information. There are combinations of keyword and keyword strategies, pegword strategies (for remembering numbered or ordered information), and combinations of keyword and pegword strategies that have been successfully implemented with students with learning disabilities across a wide range of content areas.

The previous example used English vocabulary, but this same type of procedure has been applied to learning unfamiliar social studies content, science content, and foreign language vocabulary. In all instances, the keyword strategy or combinations of the keyword strategies can be used to facilitate the learning of unfamiliar names of people, places, concepts, and events.

HOW CAN I USE MNEMONIC STRATEGIES IN MY TEACHING?

Mnemonic strategies have been developed across a variety of content domains and have proven successful with students with learning disabilities from elementary to high school grade levels. Examples across many of those content areas are now presented.

Social Studies Content Examples

Social studies content contains many unfamiliar names, places, events, and vocabulary for students with learning disabilities (Mastropieri and Scruggs, 1991). Adaptations of the keyword method have been successfully applied to student learning of varied social studies topics. For example, when learning information about the causes leading up to US involvement in World War I, students are typically required to know about the sinking of the *Lusitania* and the Zimmerman incident. Both of these major World War I events can be taught using mnemonic strategies.

To learn that the *Lusitania* was a passenger ship sunk by a German submarine and 128 Americans were killed, apply the same development principles described previously. First, create a keyword for *Lusitania*; in this case, Lucy from Charles Shultz's "Peanuts" cartoon strip would be a good concrete proxy for the *Lusitania* because it is acoustically similar, very concrete, familiar to students, and easily pictured. The interactive picture could show Lucy standing on the ship that is being sunk by a German submarine with the information about 128 Americans also being killed.

When asked to retrieve the information about the *Lusitania*, tell students to think of the keyword that sounds like *Lusitania* (Lucy) and to remember what else was happening in that picture with Lucy in it to retrieve the information. Since Lucy was standing on a ship being sunk by a German submarine and 128 Americans were killed, students retrieve that the *Lusitania* was a passenger ship that was sunk by a German submarine and 128 Americans were killed (Mastropieri and Scruggs, 1998).

As another example, a mnemonic strategy can be developed to help students recall the Zimmerman incident. This mnemonic strategy helps students learn that the Zimmerman incident referred to Germany sending a coded note to Mexico asking it to fight the United States along the Texas–Mexico border. Because that coded note was intercepted by the United States, this was a leading cause for US involvement in World War I.

In this case, the keyword *swimmer* represents Zimmerman and is shown swimming with a coded note to Mexico from Germany. The note says: "To Mexico: Join us.—Germany." When asked about the Zimmerman incident, students first retrieve the keyword "swimmer." They then think about what was happening in the picture with the swimmer in it. Finally, they retrieve the information about a coded note being sent to Mexico from Germany asking Mexico to fight the United States.

Fontana, Mastropieri, and Scruggs (2007) implemented mnemonics strategies to teach vocabulary associated with high school world history classes. Fontana developed and designed mnemonic techniques for key vocabulary identified by the inclusive high school teachers. One example includes teaching the definition of anarchist, meaning people opposed to all government. The keyword *ant* (for anarchist) was shown knocking down a dome similar to the Capitol, which represented government.

Regularly assigned teachers implemented the mnemonic instruction in their classes over several weeks, introducing only a few strategies at a time. Teachers presented the mnemonics using overhead projectors while students had small cards containing the interactive pictures for independent practice with the materials.

Marshak, Mastropieri, and Scruggs (2011) implemented mnemonic materials in classwide peer tutoring configurations to teach information about US history. Tutoring pairs worked together to learn relevant information. For example, to remember that John D. Rockefeller controlled much of the oil industry, students in pairs took turns asking each other this information. When the question was answered correctly, the tutor moved on to the next card.

If the student didn't know the answer, they were provided with a mnemonic strategy, in this case, a picture of oil (representing the oil industry) being poured on a rock (keyword for Rockefeller). After ten weeks of instruction, students using mnemonic tutoring materials substantially outperformed students in a traditional instruction condition on tested recall of social studies content.

Keyword-Keyword Strategies

Keyword strategies are ideally suited to situations where unfamiliar content is to be associated with familiar content as in the previous examples. However, when both pieces of information are unfamiliar to students, two keywords can be combined to develop a single mnemonic strategy.

For example, keyword-keyword strategies have been developed to help students learn the names of the states and their capitals (Mastropieri,

Scruggs, Bakken, and Brigham, 1992). When both the state and the capital names are unfamiliar or difficult to picture, such as Baton Rouge and Louisiana, develop keywords for both and design an interactive illustration containing both keywords doing something together. Students can be taught to retrieve the information by selecting either the state name or the capital name.

Since the capital name, Baton Rouge, and its state name, Louisiana, might be unfamiliar to many students with learning disabilities, create two interacting keywords in an interactive illustration. In this case, baton and rouge are good keywords for Baton Rouge and Louise and Anna are good keywords for Louisiana. Both keywords could be interacting in an illustration in which "Louise" and "Anna" are wearing rouge and twirling batons.

When asked what is the capital of Louisiana, prompt students to think of the keywords "Louise" and "Anna" (for Louisiana), to think back to what was happening in that picture (they were twirling batons and wearing rouge), and to retrieve Baton Rouge. When asked in the reverse order ("Baton Rouge is the capital of what state?"), prompt students to first think to the keyword for Baton Rouge (batons and rouge). Then, they should ask themselves what was happening in that picture (Louise and Anna were wearing rouge and twirling batons) and retrieve Louisiana as the state name (Louise and Anna = Louisiana).

Numbered or Ordered Information

Using Pegwords

Often, students are required to learn information that is numbered or ordered. In these cases, the use of a pegword strategy can be combined with a keyword strategy to facilitate recall. Pegwords rhyme with numbers and represent numbers that can be placed in interactive illustrations to help facilitate recall. The following are commonly used pegwords:

- One is bun.
- Two is shoe.
- Three is tree.
- Four is door (or floor).
- Five is hive.
- Six is sticks.
- Seven is heaven.
- Eight is gate.
- Nine is vine (or line).
- Ten is hen.

Pegwords are usually easy for students with learning disabilities and can be mastered by simply practicing the list a few times. Then, substitute a pegword for a number within interactive illustrations with the to-be-associated information, just as in the keyword illustrations.

For example, to learn that insects have six legs, first teach the pegword *sticks* for six, then teach students to think of an insect walking on sticks (or show an interactive illustration of the information). Finally, when asked "How many legs does an insect have?" students are taught to think of "insects" and what was happening in the picture with the insects in it, recall that the insects were walking on sticks, remember that sticks represented six, and respond with the number six. Conversely, when students are asked, "What has six legs?" prompt them to think of the pegword *sticks* for six, to remember what was happening in the picture with the sticks in it (an insect was walking on sticks), and to retrieve "insect." To help remember that spiders have eight legs, show a picture of a spider spinning a web on a gate (pegword for eight).

Pegwords can also be combined with letter strategies (in this case, acronyms) to remember relevant information. For example, to remember freedoms guaranteed in the First Amendment to the US Constitution, picture a rap singer who "raps about buns." Bun is the pegword for one, or First, Amendment, and RAPS is an acronym for the freedoms of religion, assembly, press, and speech.

Keyword-Pegword Strategies

Keywords and pegwords can be combined when learning unfamiliar information with an associated number. Many students are required to learn the order of the US presidents as part of their social studies requirements. Pegwords can be combined with keywords for learning the order of the US presidents. For example, to learn that Thomas Jefferson was the third president, use tree as the pegword for the third president (or president number 3) and chef as a good keyword for Jefferson.

Think of (or show) a picture of a "chef sitting in a tree" to help remember that Jefferson was president number three. When asked to recall the information, students can be taught to retrieve the information in two different ways. First, when asked to remember who was president number three, tell students to think of the pegword *tree* (for three) and remember what was happening in the picture with the tree in it. Since a chef was sitting in the tree, recall that "chef" represented Jefferson and therefore Jefferson was the third president of the United States.

When asked to retrieve the information in the reverse order, such as "What number president was Jefferson?" think of the keyword for Jefferson (chef) and then think of what was happening in the picture with the chef in it.

Since a chef was sitting in a tree, retrieve that tree represents three and recall that Jefferson was president number three. If all president names are unfamiliar to students such that a keyword will prompt the president name (e.g., film = Fillmore), practice the relevant presidents' names until they become more familiar.

Science Content Examples

Mnemonic strategies have also been successfully designed and implemented in the science content area (see, e.g., Scruggs, Mastropieri, Levin, and Gaffney, 1985). The principles for developing and using the strategies are identical to those described in social studies. For example, to learn that the mineral topaz is eight on the Mohs hardness scale, think of the pegword *gate* for "eight" and the keyword *top* for "topaz." Then remember a picture of a top spinning on a gate.

When asked to retrieve what number topaz is on the hardness scale, think of the keyword for topaz (top), what was happening in the picture with the top in it (spinning on a gate for eight), and retrieve eight. This mnemonic can be practiced retrieving the information the opposite way. When asked "What mineral is eight on the hardness scale?" tell students to think of the pegword for eight (gate), think back to the picture with the gate in it and what was happening (top spinning on a gate), and retrieve the answer topaz (keyword for top).

Multiple attributes. Multiple attributes can be combined within one mnemonic illustration to facilitate learning of more than one item. In learning about minerals, students may be required to learn not only the hardness level but also the color and common use of the mineral. For example, a keyword-pegword strategy can be combined as described above, but the keyword can also be colored in the actual mineral color to represent the mineral's color. In addition, the common use can be represented in an interactive fashion with the other pictorial elements.

For example, wolframite is four on the hardness scale, black in color, and is a source of tungsten for filaments used in making light bulbs. All of these pieces of information can be depicted in an interactive illustration of a "black wolf standing on a floor surrounded by light bulbs" in which black represents the color of wolframite, wolf is the keyword for wolframite, floor is the pegword for four, or the hardness level, and the light bulbs represent a common use of the mineral. Research has indicated that learning is greatly facilitated for students with learning disabilities when combinations of facts are integrated within one illustration (Scruggs et al., 1985).

Chemistry Content

Mnemonic strategies can also be designed to help facilitate the learning and memory of complex chemistry content in inclusive high school classes. The same principles are implemented, but the content level appears more complex than that for which some of the earlier mnemonics were developed (see Mastropieri and Scruggs, 2000, for additional details). Some of the information in chemistry requires learning the names and accomplishments of important people such as Mendelev.

To learn that Mendelev was the Russian who developed the first periodic table, students were taught the keyword *men dealing* for Mendelev and shown a picture of "men dealing cards from the periodic table" to represent that Mendelev developed the first periodic table of elements. Instructional steps remained similar to those described previously. When asked to retrieve who Mendelev was, students were taught to think of the keyword (men dealing) and what was happening in that picture. Once they retrieved "men dealing cards from the periodic table," they were able to remember that Mendelev was the Russian who developed the first periodic table.

Chemistry content is cumulative in nature and tends to be more abstract and complex. Students are required to learn a great deal of information about the periodic table, including the attributes associated with the general organization of the periodic table. They must know that on the periodic table, periods go across in rows and groups go up and down in columns. Mnemonics that teach those facts could include learning that (a) periods end sentences that go left to right to help remember that periods on the periodic table go left to right and (b) things grow up to help remember that groups (grow) go up and down in columns.

These mnemonics can be pictured on a smaller periodic table to help reinforce the information. In our research, additional pieces of information were continually embedded within the periodic table whenever teachers identified critical content that needed to be mastered by students. Additional characteristics about the periodic table included that (a) mass and electron affinity increase across periods; (b) size decreases across the periods; (c) reactivity and atomic radius increase across groups; (d) electron negativity decreases across groups; and (e) halogens and earth metals are examples of groups.

Peer tutoring with mnemonics in chemistry. Once students have learned the steps in mnemonic strategy instruction, they can practice those strategies independently with peers. Tutors can serve to promote recall of important terms as well as related information and meaningful verbal elaborations on the conceptual foundations of that information. The tutoring chemistry materials contain questions about the important content, mnemonic illustrations, and questions for peer tutors to ask their partners for follow-up and for related information about and elaborations on the specific content. For these materials, commercially available clip art is available to develop mnemonic illustrations.

Recent research suggests that students have worked with partners as tutoring buddies in high school inclusive chemistry classes practicing abstract chemistry content together. Reciprocal tutoring, or tutoring in which students reverse roles and serve as both tutor and tutee, was implemented (Regan, Evmenova, Mastropieri, and Scruggs, 2015). The tutoring materials contained new information and related information about a chemistry concept. Elaborative questions were included in the materials to help link additional information required for all students.

Materials were designed so that if the initial information was known, the mnemonic strategy could be skipped, and just the associated related information could be practiced. However, for use when necessary, the mnemonic strategy was embedded in the materials for students who required extra assistance in mastering the main information. To learn that a mole represents atomic weight in grams, a strategy was developed including materials tutors would see that contained tutoring directions.

For example, the first thing tutors would say is, "What is a mole?" If partners answered correctly, tutors skipped down the page and asked, "What else is important about moles?" After that question had been practiced, tutors asked, "What is an example of a mole?" If students were incorrect on the initial response, tutors presented the mnemonic strategy to help facilitate the learning. In this case, tutors said, "Think of the word *mole* (mole the animal for mole in chemistry). Now think of this picture of a 'mole on a scale looking at his weight in grams' to help you remember that a mole is the atomic weight in grams of an element." Tutoring materials contained a mnemonic interactive picture that was shown to tutees.

Following the mnemonic strategy practice, tutors proceeded to the next questions on the related information: "What else is important about moles?" and "What is an example of a mole?" Correct answers were also included on the tutoring materials and tutors continuously provided corrective feedback. Once students had completed practicing a set of about four to five strategies, students reversed roles so that each acted as a tutor and a tutee. During tutoring sessions, students had recording sheets to document the date they practiced each strategy and whether or not they had mastered the content.

Initially, all students in the tenth-grade chemistry classes checked off they had mastered the content they practiced on day 1. However, when the teacher noticed the students' responses, she said, "Since I see check marks indicating you have learned all the information, it means we are ready for a quiz, right?" Immediately following the teacher's comment, students erased the check marks in the mastered column of their checklists and indicated that they still needed practice learning the information in the materials.

This situation demonstrates the need for careful teacher monitoring during tutoring sessions when students are using materials more independently. We have seen that students sometimes have the tendency to say they have learned the information prematurely.

INDEPENDENT STUDENT GENERATION OF MNEMONIC STRATEGIES

Students can also be taught to generate their own mnemonic strategies independently (King-Sears, Mercer, and Sindelar, 1992). Initially, teachers can model the way to develop effective mnemonic strategies. Steps such as the following can be beneficial for creating mnemonic strategies: (a) identify important information; (b) generate a keyword for the unfamiliar word; (c) generate (imagine, draw, or use clip art) a picture in which the keyword is interacting with the answer; (d) practice using the strategy until the information is learned (Fulk, Mastropieri, and Scruggs, 1992).

King-Sears, Mercer, and Sindelar (1992) introduced the IT-FITS strategy to promote independent mnemonic strategy use with students with learning disabilities. Their strategy consisted of the following steps: (a) Identify the term; (b) Tell the definition of the term; (c) Find a keyword; (d) Imagine the definition doing something with the keyword; (e) Think about the definition doing something with the keyword; and (f) Study what you have imagined until you know the definition (King-Sears et al., 1992, p. 27).

Although students with learning disabilities have been taught to successfully generate mnemonic strategies independently, research findings indicate that they learn more content in shorter instructional time periods when mnemonic strategies are developed and presented by teachers (see Scruggs and Mastropieri, 1992, for an example). This does not imply that teachers should not encourage students to develop strategies independently but rather that teachers should think carefully about the allocated time for specified subject areas and the content to be covered and then make good instructional decisions regarding strategy instruction based on that information.

In other words, if there is sufficient time for students to learn to develop and generate their own strategies, encourage them to do so. However, if little instructional time is available and strategies are already developed, teach students using the previously developed strategies. Remember, once mnemonic materials are developed, they can be used again and again.

How Effective Are They?

Mnemonic strategy instruction for students with learning disabilities and other mild disabilities has been studied experimentally for almost thirty-five years. Forness et al. (1997) reported that research using mnemonic strategies had one of the largest effect sizes (1.62) in all of special education intervention research. An effect size of such a magnitude indicates that students who are taught using mnemonics perform significantly and substantially better than their peer counterparts who are being taught using other instructional procedures.

Scruggs and Mastropieri (2000) reported on the numerous experimental studies as well as the classroom applications that have been conducted by teachers of students with and without learning disabilities. Again, the findings corroborate those reported by Forness et al. (1997). Across literally dozens of studies involving more than one thousand students, students taught mnemonically remembered nearly twice as much information as students taught by other means.

Moreover, they noted that numerous teacher applications in classrooms have been implemented with parallel positive findings. One recent example demonstrated the powerful effects of using the strategies within inclusive third-grade classrooms in which students with and without disabilities benefited from instruction of vocabulary with mnemonic strategies (Uberti, Scruggs, and Mastropieri, 2003). Similar findings were reported on the use of mnemonic strategies in fourth-grade inclusive social studies classes (Mastropieri, Sweda, and Scruggs, 2000).

In both of these applications, mnemonic strategies helped improve the performance of students with learning disabilities to the level of the normally achieving students. In a recent high school application, Terrill, Scruggs, and Mastropieri (2004) reported that students learning vocabulary for the SAT, across six units of instruction, remembered 49 percent of vocabulary words using traditional instruction, but remembered 92 percent all words learned mnemonically. In all of these and other applications, both teachers and students report positive comments regarding instruction using mnemonic strategies.

Converging research evidence indicates that mnemonics are very effective for meeting one critically important aspect of school learning: memory for academic content. It has also been seen that teachers can be successful at developing and implementing these strategies, and that both teachers and students appreciate their value. In response to the student who asked, "How do they expect me to remember all this stuff?" we can answer, "With organization, practice, and mnemonic strategies!"

FINAL THOUGHTS

When developing mnemonic strategies, it is important to prioritize the content to be learned and select the key pieces of information that need to be associated before developing strategies. Think of the following as a guideline for development and instruction. First, prioritize content to be learned. Select only the most important content to be learned. Rely on your district curriculum guides and state-level standards of learning.

Second, select content to be learned that is unfamiliar to the target students. Make lists of the unfamiliar content and the to-be-associated information. For example, the content *buncombe* is to be associated with empty or insincere speech. *Lusitania* is to be associated with a passenger ship sunk by a German submarine, and *molarity* is to be associated with a concentration of a solute in a solution.

Third, create keywords that are acoustically similar, familiar, and concrete to target students. Remember to brainstorm strategies, and remember also that you get better at creating keywords with practice!

Fourth, create interactive illustrations of the keywords and the to-be-remembered information. The illustrations can be drawn by hand (they don't have to be "artistic," just recognizable), created with cutouts from magazines, or drawn by an artistic student. Remember also that clip art can help with the development of almost any picture. Clip art with thousands of illustrations is available commercially or can be found on the internet for free by using a search engine and typing in "clip art" and the name of the picture you need.

Fifth, introduce the materials to your students. Provide ample opportunities for students to practice using the strategies. Monitor their strategy usage, as practicing one time will probably be insufficient. Mnemonics are usually very effective, but like any learning task, they must be practiced until they are mastered.

Sixth, teach students how to use the strategy independently. When presenting new information, say to students, "This information is important to remember, so what is a good strategy we can use to remember it?" Encourage students to practice learning and retrieving the information using the strategies.

Finally, remember mnemonic strategies such as keywords, pegwords, and combinations of them have proven successful with students with learning disabilities across a range of age/grade levels and across many content areas including vocabulary, foreign language learning, science, and social studies.

POINTS TO REMEMBER

- *Memory enhancing strategies, called mnemonic devices, help make unfamiliar information concrete.*
- *Mnemonic devices link new information with prior knowledge using visual and auditory cues.*

- *These memory strategies have proven very successful across all content areas and are backed by decades of research.*
- *Keyword and pegword strategies are used to link unfamiliar words and/or numbers. In the case of numbers, pegwords contain a rhyme, such as one is bun.*
- *Once the initial concepts are understood, peer tutoring allows students to practice semi-independently. Educators must monitor to ensure completion of activity.*

The primary author can be reached at mmastrop@gmu.edu.

REFERENCES

Fontana, J., Mastropieri, M. A., and Scruggs, T. E. (2007). Mnemonic strategy instruction in inclusive secondary social studies classes. *Remedial and Special Education,* 28, 345–55. https://doi.org/10.1177/07419325070280060401.

Forness, S. R., Kavale, K. A., Blum, B. M., and Lloyd, J. (1997). Mega-analysis of meta-analyses: What works in special education and related services. *Teaching Exceptional Children,* 29(6), 4–9. https://doi.org/10.1177/004005999702900601.

Fulk, B. J. M., Mastropieri, M. A., and Scruggs, T. E. (1992). Mnemonic generalization training with learning disabled adolescents. *Learning Disabilities Research and Practice,* 7, 2–10. Retrieved from https://eric.ed.gov/?id=EJ439568.

King-Sears, M. E., Mercer, C. D., and Sindelar, P. (1992). Toward independence with keyword mnemonics: A strategy for science vocabulary instruction. *Remedial and Special Education,* 13, 22–33. https://doi.org/10.1177/074193259201300505.

Marshak, L., Mastropieri, M. A., and Scruggs, T. E. (2011). Curriculum enhancements for inclusive secondary social studies classes. *Exceptionality,* 19 (2), 61–74. https://doi.org/10.1080/09362835.2011.562092.

Mastropieri, M. A., and Scruggs, T. E. (1991). *Teaching students ways to remember: Strategies for learning mnemonically.* Cambridge, MA: Brookline Books.

———. (1998). Constructing more meaningful relationships in the classroom: Mnemonic research into practice. *Learning Disabilities Research and Practice,* 13, 138–145. Retrieved from https://eric.ed.gov/?id=EJ571938.

———. (2000). *The inclusive classroom: Strategies for effective instruction.* Columbus, OH: Prentice-Hall/Merrill.

———. (2018). *The inclusive classroom: Strategies for effective differentiated instruction.* 6th ed. Boston: Prentice Hall.

Mastropieri, M. A., Scruggs, T. E., Bakken, J. P., and Brigham, F. J. (1992). A complex mnemonic strategy for teaching states and capitals: Comparing forward and backward associations. *Learning Disabilities Research and Practice,* 7, 96–103. Retrieved from https://eric.ed.gov/?id=EJ443023.

Mastropieri, M. A., Scruggs, T. E., and Fulk, B. J. M. (1990). Teaching abstract vocabulary with the keyword method: Effects on recall and comprehension. *Journal of Learning Disabilities,* 23, 92–96. https://doi.org/10.1177/002221949002300203.

Mastropieri, M. A., Scruggs, T. E., and Marshak, L. (2008). Training teachers, parents, and peers to implement effective teaching strategies for content area learning. In T. E. Scruggs and M. A. Mastropieri (eds.), *Personnel preparation: Advances in learning and behavioral disabilities* (vol. 21, pp. 311–29). Oxford, UK: Emerald.

Mastropieri, M. A., Sweda, J., and Scruggs, T. E. (2000). Putting mnemonic strategies to work in an inclusive classroom. *Learning Disabilities Research and Practice,* 15, 69–74. Retrieved from https://eric.ed.gov/?id=EJ608054.

Regan, K., Evmenova, A., Mastropieri, M. A., and Scruggs, T. E. (2015). Peer interactions in the content areas: Using differentiated instruction strategies. In K. R. Harris, and L. Meltzer (eds.), *The power of peers: Enhancing learning, development and social skills* (pp. 33–68). New York: Guilford.

Scruggs, T. E., and Mastropieri, M. A. (1992). Classroom applications of mnemonic instruction: Acquisition, maintenance, and generalization. *Exceptional Children,* 58, 219–29. https://doi.org/10.1177/001440299105800305.

———. (2000). The effectiveness of mnemonic instruction for students with learning and behavior problems: An update and research synthesis. *Journal of Behavioral Education,* 10, 163–73. Retrieved from https://link.springer.com/article/10.1023%2FA%3A1016640214368.

Scruggs, T. E., Mastropieri, M. A., Levin, J. R., and Gaffney, J. S. (1985). Facilitating the acquisition of science facts in learning disabled students. *American Educational Research Journal,* 22, 575–86. https://doi.org/10.3102/00028312022004575.

Terrill, C., Scruggs, T. E., and Mastropieri, M. A. (2004). SAT vocabulary instruction for high school students with learning disabilities. *Intervention in School and Clinic,* 39, 288–94. https://doi.org/10.1177/10534512040390050501.

Uberti, H. Z., Scruggs, T. E., and Mastropieri, M. A. (2003). Keywords make the difference! Mnemonic instruction in inclusive classrooms. *Teaching Exceptional Children,* 35, 3, 56–61. https://doi.org/10.1177/004005990303500308.

Yates, F. (1956). *The art of memory.* Chicago: University of Chicago Press.

Chapter Six

Student Learning Profiles

Teaching with Style in Mind

Lynne M. Celli, *Endicott College,* and Nicholas D. Young, *American International College*

The intersection of learning profiles/learning styles and the research about learning disabilities is an area of critical importance for all administrators and teachers in PreK–12 education. A learning profile/learning style is often referred to as one's strong preference for taking in, processing, and mastering new information and knowledge (McCarthy, 2014). If focusing on individual learning styles were made a major goal of every school and classroom and implemented appropriately, such focus would ensure student success.

The variable that affects the understanding of student learning profiles/styles is an emphasis on learning disability diagnoses, as often teachers confuse a possible learning disability with differing learning profiles/styles (NA-SET, n.d.). Because of the integration of these two important concepts in the classroom, attention must be squarely focused where they intersect in the teaching and learning process.

It is imperative that there be a clear and expert understanding of students' learning profiles/styles in order to link application to appropriate accommodations for students with learning disabilities, keeping in mind that they process information differently than that of their nondisabled peers (Alexander and Young, 2015; McCarthy, 2014).

This premise is not different from teachers' overall understanding of students without a diagnosed learning disability, what these students' learning profiles/learnings styles might be, and how this data must inform all pedagogy. There are some overarching approaches to teaching strategies, therefore, that are applicable to all students with or without a learning disability (Ford, 2013; Alexander and Young, 2015; Washoe County School District, 2015).

LEARNING PROFILES/LEARNING STYLES AND THE RELATIONSHIP TO LEARNING DISABILITIES

An understanding and mastery of skill application regarding student learning profiles/styles as teachers plan, implement, and evaluate classroom activities must be a focus to ensure the learning success of all students. Every student, in every classroom, has a unique learning style sometimes characterized as auditory, visual, and tactile/kinesthetic that must be addressed with appropriate pedagogy in all content areas (Morgan, 2013; Celli and Young, 2014).

How students take in, process, master, and apply information also affects students diagnosed with learning disabilities, as their learning processes are often not the same (Edutopia, 2016; Sturomski, 2017). Thus, a thorough review of variables with reference to understanding learning profiles/learning styles and how they interface with the educational needs of students with learning disabilities becomes a critical foundational skill set for every teacher.

Educators who truly want to excel at their craft must always be on the forefront of best practice and the elements of teaching for academic success for all students. Teachers must also understand that students with learning disabilities process new information much differently than their typical general education peers, and need pedagogy different than that of students without disabilities, which is similar to understanding learning profiles/learning styles (Sturomski, 2017; Washoe County School District, 2015).

It is a natural next step, then, to integrate learning profiles/learning styles research with proven learning disabilities research, as both relate to student success. The importance of multifaceted learning profiles/learning styles dictates that teachers who work with students with learning disabilities must learn to incorporate this research into much-needed modifications and accommodations to improve student outcomes (Washoe County School District, 2015; Ford, 2013).

LEARNING SUCCESS FOR ALL STUDENTS

The Auditory Learner

Understanding the academic needs of auditory learners in the classroom will assist teachers in mastering the skills necessary to adapt their own pedagogy, thereby addressing the learning styles of both the auditory learner and peers with learning disabilities who display similar qualities (Dyslexia Victoria,

2017; Celli and Young, 2014). Auditory learners have several unique characteristics, including a profound ability to learn by hearing and conceptualizing information, focusing on the task at hand, connecting pieces of information to understand a whole concept, and memorizing information (Celli and Young, 2014; UMass Dartmouth, 2017).

These learners are analytical and use common sense; they excel at being able to understand a concept that is subjective and raising it to the objective, comparing and classifying, predicting, reaching final thoughts, and understanding the full concepts, as well as the supporting details (Boundless, 2016). Further, auditory learners must understand the purpose and ultimate goal of lessons/activities/units of study, which should be clearly stated and outlined at the outset.

Connecting auditory style with learning disabilities. With the research regarding auditory learners and students with learning disabilities in mind, there are some specific teaching strategies that ensure success for these students, as well as students who need to enhance this type of learning style (Prichard, 2018). Educators need to keep these strategies in mind when planning, implementing, and evaluating effectiveness of all lessons and activities.

These research-based teaching strategies for the auditory learner include basic direct instruction or lecture, whole-group or small-group discussion, providing the opportunity for oral demonstration of mastery, and providing the opportunity for work that requires memorization to show mastery (Celli and Young, 2014; Prichard, 2018). Pedagogy that includes programmed instruction; very clear objectives that have built-in time for practice; tasks that require specific, targeted answers; and modeling of higher-order thinking skills are strategies that complement an auditory learner's style and will assist in showing mastery of new skills and new knowledge (UMassDartmouth, 2017; Sturomski, 2017).

Utilizing these teaching strategies will also assist students whose preferred learning style is not auditory as it will provide practice and the opportunity to strengthen this nonpreferred style. To connect the preferred teaching strategies of the auditory learner with the learning needs of students with learning disabilities, it is also recommended that educators provide very direct instructions, similar to the auditory learners' needs.

Being explicit about expectations with both the typical auditory learner as well as students with learning disabilities has proven to be a very successful teaching strategy, and similarly, systematic and sequential instruction works well for students that are auditory by nature as well as for students with a learning disability in the area of processing (Prichard, 2018; Ford, 2013).

By approaching teaching in a very sequential way, auditory learners and students with challenges in processing will be able to access curricula, new information, and new knowledge in a step-by-step manner (Ezekiel, 2017). This allows for understanding, processing, and eventual mastery of this new information and new knowledge by interacting with it in small steps, rather than trying to learn and master a whole concept.

Adding the strategy of precise questioning to the above skill set also provides educators and students with clarification information as well as formative, ongoing assessment to measure student understanding of the smaller parts of a concept, and thus inform future activities and lessons with useful data. Integrating similar strategies that will address the learning strengths of auditory learners will also address many of the challenges of students diagnosed with learning disabilities in areas such as processing and retaining information (Ford, 2013; Washoe County School District, 2015).

The Visual Learner

When educators adapt pedagogy to understand and address the learning needs of the visual learner and student with similar learning disabilities, successful learning is the most logical outcome. Visual learners have distinctive learning characteristics and because of the emphasis most schools place on the presentation of new information and new knowledge in a verbal or auditory way, they may experience difficulty in learning (Celli and Young, 2014).

Visual learners represent the largest number of learners in any group at 65 percent; therefore, visual learners must have the opportunity to interact visually with this new information and new knowledge (Busan, 2014). These learners view concepts from the whole concepts and proceed to parse them down into the individual components that make up complete concept for understanding. Demonstration that encourages the use of students' "mind's eye" pedagogy benefits these learners (Boundless, 2016).

Visual learners excel when given the chance to have a learning environment that has visual learning cues and stimuli, and social cues; thus, they respond best with group work where they can share and provide understanding of their new learning with pictures and outlines (Celli and Young, 2014). A multisensory approach to teaching strategies as well as planning lessons and activities that require students to exhibit new learning in various ways—most importantly being able to illustrate what they have learned—is critical (Ezekiel, 2017).

For this type of student, the best learning occurs when they are presented with the chance to make a mental image or visualize the new learning that needs to occur. This allows the learning to be holistic and internalized as the whole concept. The student benefits from a classroom with global organization, as defined by much external stimuli, always connected to current learning as well as allowing them to consistently "experience" the environment (Prichard, 2018). Due to their short attention spans, visual learners need external stimuli that enhances engagement, which will, in turn, also enhance overall learning.

Connecting visual style with learning disabilities. There are specific teaching strategies that help visual learners and those with learning disabilities. It is important that educators keep these in mind when planning, implementing, and evaluating the effectiveness of lessons and activities.

Visual learners and students with learning disabilities need a holistic approach of pedagogy that includes the use of graphic organizers, use of webbing to provide a concrete visual aid, modeling of how to interface with the new learning skills, offering student choice of how they want to complete lessons and activities, and encouraging creativity in exhibiting mastery of skills (Dyslexia Victoria, 2017; Celli and Young, 2014).

Further, research-based teaching practices that include computer-aided instruction and activities and lessons that encourage thinking outside the box and that are open-ended allow both the visual learner and the student diagnosed with a learning disability (such as processing difficulties, language disabilities, or executive functioning issues) the chance to show mastery in alternative ways (Prichard, 2018; Celli and Young, 2014).

Teaching strategies that also include the use of external stimuli as an integral part of the learning process not only promotes academic success for these types of learners, it also dispels the myth that teaching to the senses and asking for response in the same manner are not appropriate, research-based strategies (Prichard, 2018).

It is also of importance that educators specifically assess how students respond to the external stimuli provided in planned lessons, and if this indeed assists in positive learning success and mastery of new knowledge and new information. This type of external stimuli, however, should not include outside noise such as music as this type of outside stimuli not only interferes with the visual learner but also confuses the learning-disabled student (Edutopia, 2016; Sturomski, 2018).

Utilizing these teaching strategies will also assist students whose preferred learning style is not visual, providing practice and an opportunity to strengthen this nonpreferred style. To connect the favored teaching strategies of the visual learner with the learning needs of students with learning disabilities, it is recommended that teachers circulate throughout the classroom and provide concrete and immediate feedback on work that students are attending to (Prichard, 2018; Ford, 2013).

Visual learners and peers with learning disabilities who exhibit similar traits access academics best with pictures, whether real pictures or learning to use visual imaging in the student's mind's eye. This strategy must be modeled by teachers as it is not automatically mastered by all students. Another typical characteristic of this type of learner is that they do not respond well to structures and compartmentalized learning, nor do they respond well to timed activities or lessons (Boundless, 2016).

The goal is for these students is to exhibit mastery through untimed activities, lessons, and tests, providing an environment where students feel at ease when progressing through work without the pressure to rush through anything (Washoe County School District, 2015). All of the above research-based pedagogy must be implemented to ensure the academic success of visual learners and their learning-disabled counterparts (Prichard, 2018; Alexander and Young, 2015).

The Tactile/Kinesthetic Learner

Tactile/kinesthetic learners have very distinctive learning characteristics, just as auditory and visual learners possess, and understanding the needs of these students helps to adapt educator pedagogy for the classroom. However, these tactile/kinesthetic learners represent the smallest number of students in any given classroom at only 5 percent; therefore, the specific learning needs of these students are often overlooked and rarely addressed (Celli and Young, 2014; Ezekiel, 2017).

These learners are frequently misunderstood and often referred for special education testing, as their need for movement and experiential learning is often confused with conditions such as attention deficit hyperactivity disorder (ADHD), autism, or behavior issues. These learners prefer an active, hands-on, project-based approach to learning (Griss, 2013; Gilakjani, 2012).

There is relatively little research regarding the learning needs appropriate for tactile/kinesthetic learners; therefore, teachers must be vigilant in learning and understanding pedagogy necessary for learning success for this population of students, as traditional schools and classrooms are arranged in a way that primarily use auditory pedagogy, which is diametrically opposite of the learning needs of the tactile/kinesthetic learners (Griss, 2013).

Traditional schools and classrooms are rarely arranged to include an informal design for learning, which is a critical component of the learning success for tactile/kinesthetic learners. Further, teachers, through no fault of their own, are often less familiar with teaching strategies that address the learning needs of tactile/kinesthetic learners (Awla, 2014; Gilakjani, 2012).

These students must have opportunities to move frequently and interact with artifacts related to learning new concepts, moving from whole to part with regard to new concepts. This is similar to the visual learners. This knowledge is key for teachers as they plan, implement, and evaluate lessons and activities for tactile/kinesthetic learners (Awla, 2014).

Teaching strategies that include preplanned activities and lessons that are communicated to tactile/kinesthetic learners in advance are proven to be effective for learning success. These types of activities and lessons provide opportunities for tactile/kinesthetic learners to show mastery of new knowledge and information by physically interacting with learning artifacts (Ezekiel, 2017; Prichard, 2018). This scenario combined with expected and approved movement in the classroom and during lessons is critical for these students to experience academic learning success (Celli and Young, 2014).

Students learn best when they are presented with environments that are compatible with their preferred learning style (Hoover, 2012). This puts tactile/kinesthetic learners at a distinct disadvantage, since most teachers are not equipped or trained to adjust pedagogy that ensures academic success for these students. Tactile learners are ever conscious of space; thus, the organization of learning space to allow for movement—which is not common in a typical classroom—is a must (Griss, 2013).

For tactile/kinesthetic learners, the best learning occurs when they are presented with the choice of how and when to move and activities that have practical application to life experiences to make a mental image or visualize the learning that needs to occur (UMass Dartmouth, 2017). Often referred to as having a strong motor memory, this is a successful strategy since tactile/visual learners can remember things once they have "done" them.

Integration between the process of moving and interacting with the whole learning environment in a way that these learners are most comfortable produces the biggest gains for kinesthetic learners as they benefit from classrooms where they can consistently "experience" the environment (Prichard, 2018). Since tactile/kinesthetic learners sometimes appear to be daydreaming, fidget, and often tend to have short attention spans, learning environments that recognize these learning needs allow for the best opportunity for learning success (Ezekiel, 2017; Griss, 2013).

Connecting kinesthetic style with learning disabilities. There are many instructional strategies that aid learning for visual and auditory learners; however, there are far fewer that are clear and as easily implemented for tactile/kinesthetic learners (Griss, 2013). This is also the case for connecting pedagogy for tactile/kinesthetic learners diagnosed with learning disabilities that exhibit similar learning needs and teaching styles to tactile/kinesthetic learners (Awla, 2014; Gilakjani, 2012).

It is worth repeating that teachers must be mindful of these strategies, planning and implementing activities and lessons with the needs of students diagnosed with learning disabilities in mind. These students may present with diagnoses such as difficulty processing, ADHD, behaviors similar to students with autism learning needs, and behavior issues similar to the visual learners' needs (Ford, 2013). Students diagnosed with processing or comprehension learning disabilities may exhibit behaviors such as daydreaming, doodling, or simply not paying attention to the activity or lesson at hand (Ford, 2013).

Similar teaching strategies such as redirecting students to tasks at hand and by allowing for group work not only at a table but also in an open-ended way help the learning-disabled student. Creating ways students can physically touch something during a lesson addresses the learning needs of both groups. These learners have an intuitive nature to focus on copying what they see; thus, modeling is a great strategy for these learners (Griss, 2013; Ezekiel, 2017).

Best practice suggests that teachers should routinely show students, step by step, exactly what is expected of them; for example, modeling the exact learning expectations and how to reach the goal(s) of activities/lessons (Awla, 2014). With the research regarding learning success for the tactile/kinesthetic learner and students with learning disabilities in mind, one important point to keep in mind is that these students may purposely create situations during an activity or lesson so they can provide themselves with the movement they need to be successful (Gilakjani, 2011).

An example of student-initiated movement breaks might be asking to sharpen a pencil or use the bathroom often, or deliberately dropping a book so they can have the chance to move to retrieve it. These behaviors should be triggers or red flags for teachers that they need to be more attentive to the learning needs of both the tactile/kinesthetic learner and students diagnosed with learning disabilities that have similar learning needs (Awla, 2014; Boundless, 2016). These research-based teaching strategies for tactile/kinesthetic learners are critical to ensure academic success for these students.

Teachers must continually assess how students respond to the external stimuli provided in planned lessons and evaluate whether this indeed inhibits positive learning success and mastery of new knowledge and new information (Prichard, 2018). This type of external stimuli that is directly related to an activity or lesson should not include outside noise such as music, as it interferes with the concentration of the tactile/kinesthetic learner and also confuses the learning-disabled student diagnosed with similar learning needs (Griss, 2013).

The lecture and student note-taking pedagogy that teachers often implement actually sets the tactile/kinesthetic learner up for failure. These teaching strategies actually run counter to the tactile/kinesthetic learner's need to be able to interact with learning and go through the steps required to reach an academic goal; thus, they should be avoided at all cost (Awla, 2014).

FINAL THOUGHTS

Recent PreK–12 education has become heavily focused on accountability and designing, implementing, and evaluating schools and individual classrooms that ensure academic success for all students. In many states, teacher evaluations are now being tied to student learning and mastery of new knowledge; therefore, the intersection of learning profiles/learning styles is an area of critical importance of focus for all administrators and teachers.

Utilizing multifaceted teaching strategies specific to each learning style—auditory, visual, or tactile/kinesthetic—will not only provide classroom activities and lessons geared for academic success, but continued practice in the nonpreferred areas will strengthen student learning overall. Further, by diversifying teaching pedagogy with learning styles research in mind, educators are able to address the academic needs of students diagnosed with learning disabilities.

Examples of these types of learning disabilities include such areas as language, processing, attention deficit hyperactivity disorder, and executive functioning, as well as what may be interpreted as behavior issues. When connecting teaching strategies of students with many different learning needs, it is also recommended that educators circulate throughout the classroom and provide concrete and immediate feedback on work that students are attending to, for all learners.

A thorough understanding of students diagnosed with learning disabilities who exhibit the same needs as their learning styles counterparts ensures educators are using a plethora of strategies that are targeted for academic success. Integrating varied strategies will address the learning strengths of each type of student as well as mitigate many of the challenges of students diagnosed with learning disabilities. Educators must use research-based pedagogy for the visual, auditory, and kinesthetic learner, as well as the learning-disabled student, to ensure the academic success for all students.

POINTS TO REMEMBER

- *Learning profiles are the specific way each person takes in, processes, and masters new information and knowledge.*
- *Understanding individual learning styles allows educators to differentiate instruction, thus meeting the needs of all learners, especially students with learning disabilities.*
- *Students with learning disabilities process information differently than nondisabled peers, thus requiring a different pedagogy.*
- *The auditory, tactile, and verbal learners all have unique learning traits as well as some similarities.*
- *The educator of students with learning disabilities needs to continually assess and rework lessons and assessments to ensure student needs are being met.*

The primary author can be reached at cellilynne@aol.com.

REFERENCES

Alexander, J. S., and Young, N. D. (2015). Applying the response to intervention framework to reading challenges: A multifaceted approach. In N. D. Young and C. N. Michael (eds.), *Beyond the Bedtime Story: Promoting Reading Development during the Middle Years* (pp. 97–108). Lanham, MD: Rowman & Littlefield.

Awla, H. A. (2014). Learning styles and their relation to teaching styles. Retrieved from http://article.sciencepublishinggroup.com/pdf/10.11648.j.ijll.20140203.23.pdf.

Boundless. (2016). Effective teaching strategies. *Boundless Education*. Retrieved from https://www.boundless.com/education/textbooks/boundless-education-textbook/working-with-students-4/teaching-strategies-21/effective-teaching-strategies-64-12994/.

Busan, A.-M. (2014). Learning styles of medical students: Implications for educators. Retrieved from https://www.ncbi.nlm.nih.gov/pubmed/25729590.

Celli, L., and Young, N. D. (2014). *Learning styles perspectives: Impact in the classroom*. 3rd ed. Madison, WI: Atwood.

Dyslexia Victoria. (2017). Learning styles (auditory, visual, and kinesthetic) and dyslexics. Retrieved from http://www.dyslexiavictoriaonline.com/learning-style-auditory-visual-kinesthetic-dyslexics/.

Edutopia. (2016). Multiple intelligences: What does the research say? *Edutopia*. Retrieved from https://www.edutopia.org/multiple-intelligences-research.

Ezekiel, R. (2017). Studying style: What's your personal learning style? Retrieved from https://www.studyingstyle.com/.

Finley, T. (2015). Are learning styles real—and useful? *Edutopia*. Retrieved from https://www.edutopia.org/article/learning-styles-real-and-useful-todd-finley.

Ford, J. (2013). Educating students with learning disabilities in inclusive classrooms. Retrieved from http://corescholar.libraries.wright.edu/cgi/viewcontent.cgi?article=1154&context=ejie.

Gilakjani, A. P. (2012). A match or mismatch between learning styles of student's and teaching styles of teachers. Retrieved from http://www.mecs-press.net/ijmecs/ijmecs-v4-n11/IJMECS-V4-N11-5.pdf.

Griss, G. (2013). The power of movement in teaching and learning. Retrieved from http://www.edweek.org/tm/articles/2013/03/19/fp_griss.html.

Hoover, J. J. (2012). Reducing unnecessary referral: Guidelines for teachers of diverse learners. *Teaching Exceptional Children*, 44(4), 38–47. Retrieved from http://journals.sagepub.com/doi/abs/10.1177/004005991204400404.

Kolb, A. Y., and Kolb, D. A. (2008). Experiential theory: A dynamic, holistic approach to management learning, education, and development. In S. J. Armstrong and C. Fukami (eds.), *Handbook of Management and Development*. London: Sage.

McCarthy, J. (2014). How learning profiles can strengthen your teaching. *Edutopia*. Retrieved from https://www.edutopia.org/blog/learning-profiles-john-mccarthy.

Morgan, S. (2013). *Motivating students—carrot or stick?* DOI: 10.1111.vnj.12006.

NASET. (n.d.). Characteristics of children with learning disabilities. Retrieved from http://www.naset.org/fileadmin/user_upload/LD_Report/Issue__3_LD_Report_Characteristic_of_LD.pdf.

Prichard, A. (2018). *Ways of learning: Learning theories for the classroom* (4th ed). New York, NY: Routledge.

Sturomski, N. (2017). Teaching student with learning disabilities to use learning strategies. Retrieved from http://neilsturomski.com/teaching-students-with-learning-disabilities-to-use-learning-strategies/.

UMass Dartmouth. (2017). Tips for educators on accommodating different learning styles. Retrieved from http://www.umassd.edu/dss/resources/facultystaff/howtoteachandaccommodate/howtoaccommodatedifferentlearningstyles/.

Washoe County School District. (2015). Student learning objectives: Instructional strategies list. Retrieved from https://www.washoeschools.net/cms/lib08/NV01912265/Centricity/Domain/228/Instructional%20Strategies%20List%20July%202015.pdf.

Chapter Seven

Instructional Strategies to Support the Writing Process for Students with Learning Disabilities as Well as Struggling Writers

Nicholas D. Young, *American International College,* and Kristen Bonanno-Sotiropoulos, *Bay Path University*

The Common Core State Standards place great emphasis on proficiency in written expression for all learners, including those with disabilities. Proficiency in writing and well-developed writing skills are a requirement for graduation and beyond, as heavily evidenced by high-stakes testing and college acceptance guidelines (Flanagan and Bouck, 2015; Mason, Harris, and Graham, 2011; Troia and Olinghouse, 2013). Alarming statistics reveal that, while an estimated 27 percent of students in grades 8 and 12 are proficient or higher in writing, an overwhelming 74 percent are below the proficiency level (Harris and Graham, 2013; National Center for Education Statistics, 2012).

To be identified as an evidence-based practice, a process has to be backed by extensive research and shown to produce positive results (Graham, Harris, and Chambers, 2016; Harris et al., 2017). In order for teachers to consistently implement evidence-based practices, they must first become knowledgeable in identifying them. When teachers are knowledgeable in recognizing evidence-based practices, they become more conscious of choosing what instructional support is best for their students (Graham et al., 2016).

The writing process involves multifaceted capabilities and skills that produce challenges for students with learning disabilities (Harris and Graham,

2013; Johnson, Hancock, Carter, and Pool, 2012; Troia and Olinghouse, 2013). Spelling accuracy, organizing thoughts, grammar, punctuation, and handwriting are components of written expression that can be affected by a learning disability (Connelly, Dockrell, and Lindsay, 2009).

Through implementation of evidence-based writing strategies, educators can provide support for academic gains for students with learning disabilities (Harris et al., 2017). Explicit instruction in spelling and word patterns, teaching of self-regulation strategy development, and incorporation of a writer's workshop model are all evidence-based writing practices.

Students with learning disabilities (LD) often experience frustration and a lack of motivation to write due to the high level of cognitive, linguistic, affective, and behavioral tasks required within the process of writing (Troia and Olinghouse, 2013). Through the use of evidence-based writing strategies, teachers can support self-regulation skills and increase writing motivation while teaching critical components of writing.

EDUCATIONAL LEGISLATION AND COMMON CORE STATE STANDARDS

The best way to close the achievement gap is through the consistent use of evidence-based instructional practices. The Individuals with Disabilities Education Improvement Act of 2004 (IDEIA) and the Every Student Succeeds Act (formerly No Child Left Behind Act of 2001) mandate the use of evidence-based or research-based instructional practices to improve student outcomes.

The adoption of the Common Core State Standards places a heavy emphasis on written expression, thus encouraging the use of evidence-based teaching practices in the area of writing. However, the lack of teacher training, insufficient resources, and limited research on writing practices contribute to the slow progression of widespread evidence-based writing strategies (Gilbert and Graham, 2010; Troia and Olinghouse, 2013). In addition, under IDEIA, the implementation of research-based interventions is required to be used within a Response to Intervention (RTI) framework as well as support the identification of a learning disability (Troia, 2013).

HOW THE WRITING PROCESS IS AFFECTED WHEN A LEARNING DISABILITY IS PRESENT

According to the Individuals with Disabilities Education Improvement Act of 2004, a specific learning disability is one that involves a disorder of one of several psychological processes that causes a defect in the ability to read, write, spell, think, speak or complete computations (American Speech-

Language-Hearing Association, 2017). Inaccuracies in spelling and deficits in writing fluency are the most prevalent weaknesses for students with learning disabilities (Harris et al., 2017).

Students who fail to master the foundational skills required for reading will likely struggle with writing development (Connelly et al., 2009). Throughout the writing process, students with learning disabilities may experience setbacks with organizing ideas, planning, expressing their thoughts, and revising their work (Harris and Graham, 2013; Mason et al., 2011).

Writing involves cognitive, linguistic, affective, and behavioral tasks working in unison. For students with learning disabilities, this can prove to be exasperating and as a result can hinder progress within the writing process (Troia and Olinghouse, 2013). Students with learning disabilities display deficits in working memory, which play a critical role in the ability to utilize multiple cognitive tasks (Berninger, Lee, Abbott, and Breznitz, 2013).

Graham and Santangelo (2014) stress the importance of reducing a student's concentration of directly putting thoughts into words and rather focus their understanding on the writing process. Students with LD are more likely to devote extensive energy on transcription skills such as spelling, which can result in forgetting ideas and thoughts held within the working memory (Harris et al., 2017).

Dyslexia, language learning disorders, and development coordination disorders are three specific disorders that fall under the umbrella of learning disabilities. These three disorders can negatively affect the writing process (Connelly et al., 2009). Difficulty with rapid letter naming, phonological aspects of reading and spelling, as well as impediments in spelling directly affect written expression for individuals with dyslexia (Connelly et al., 2009; Nation, 2011).

A language learning disorder (LLD), also known as a specific language impairment, impacts the processing of language. Students struggle with expressing ideas, vocabulary acquisition, spelling, comprehension, and understanding left to right (American Speech Language Hearing Association, n.d.). Development coordination disorder (DCD) hinders the use of coordinated motor skills, such as handwriting. When students struggle with handwriting, the writing process is compromised (Connelly et al., 2009).

EVIDENCE-BASED WRITING STRATEGIES

Explicit Spelling Instruction

Harris et al. (2017) claim that students with LD struggle tremendously with spelling; therefore, explicit spelling instruction is a critical component of any writing curriculum. Explicit instruction refers to direct instruction that incorporates supports and scaffolding for individual student needs. The goal of explicit instruction is to provide direct instruction until the student can master the task/skill independently. The three components to effective delivery of explicit instruction include clear statements of the purpose for learning the skill, clear explanations and modeling of the skill by the teacher, and providing supportive practice along with continuous feedback to the student (Archer and Hughes, 2011).

Students with LD need to be able to correctly and automatically spell common words that appear in writing (Harris et al., 2017). Even a relatively small number of words can have an impact on a student's ability to increase his or her writing output. To support this claim, Graham (1999) suggests that approximately 100 words account for 50 percent of the words students use in their actual writing assignments and that approximately 1,000 words account for 89 percent of student writing assignments.

Weekly spelling lists expose students to new words and should consist of ten to twenty words depending on the student's age and ability level. Spelling lists can highlight such things as different spelling patterns and sight words, and can be individualized to fit the unique needs of the student. There are three instructional strategies for assisting students with learning new spelling words: tracing and visualizing, the use of spelling games, and collaborative peer studying.

Tracing and visualizing is a strategy where students say the spelling word while either tracing the letters or visualizing the letters in their head to get a feel for the spelling of the word. While writing the word, students say each letter out loud, checking to make sure the word is spelled correctly; if not, the student corrects the spelling.

Spelling games provide another option for teaching new spelling words. Engaging in learning activities that are enjoyable may increase motivation for students. Playing spelling games should occur after students have had time to study and learn their new spelling words; therefore, spelling games can serve as a reinforcer.

Collaborative peer studying is yet another strategy proven effective at increasing students' vocabularies. In this strategy, students are paired up and throughout the week spend an allotted amount of time tutoring each other in learning the weekly spelling words (Harris et al., 2017). Students can use hand-made flash cards, whiteboards, technology, or any other number of tools to work together.

In addition to explicitly teaching students to spell, students need to understand the structure of the English language. One efficient way to teach this skill is through word sorting where students identify rules of the English language through spelling patterns and sounds. *Words Their Way* (Bear, Invernizzi, Templeton, and Johnston, 2015) is a well-known and often used word sorting program that offers a vast number of word-sort workbooks, allowing teachers to be creative and differentiate their instruction, activities, and assessment to meet individual student needs (Bear et al., 2015).

Self-Regulation Strategy Development

Helping students with learning disabilities to develop writing skills while increasing motivation can be accomplished through the use of self-regulation strategy development (SRSD), an evidence-based approach. Extensive research has proven the impact of the SRSD instructional approach on writing development for students with learning disabilities, students with attention deficit hyperactivity disorder (ADHD), as well as students who simply struggle with writing (Harris and Graham, 2013; Taft and Mason, 2011).

Explicit instruction along with opportunities for guided practice are at the heart of SRSD. Direct instruction is setting goals, self-monitoring and self-instruction techniques, as well as self-reinforcement as these are critical to the success of SRSD (Ennis, Jolivette, Terry, Frederick, and Alberto, 2015; Harris et al., 2017). Implementation of the SRSD instructional approach incorporates six stages, including building background knowledge, discussion of writing strategies, teacher modeling of the strategies, supported practice of the strategy to encourage memorization, support, and independent practice (Ennis et al., 2015; De La Paz and Sherman, 2013).

Writer's Workshop

An instructional mode that focuses on the process of writing rather than the finished project is known as Writer's Workshop (Gair, 2015; Troia, 2013). A Writer's Workshop model combines several elements. These elements include a structured routine with high expectations, teacher modeling, differentiated instruction, opportunities for conferencing with the teacher and peers, ongoing feedback, and cooperative learning environments (Gair, 2015; Troia, 2013; Wiley and McKernan, 2016).

Research has indicated positive outcomes from implementation of Writer's Workshop for students with learning disabilities and with students who struggle with writing (Troia, 2013). Through the use of a Writer's Workshop model, there is an emphasis placed upon not only the writing process but community building as well. The concept of self-selected partners and groups, as well as publicly sharing finished products, encourage and support the idea of classroom communities (Gair, 2015; Troia, 2013).

Writer's Workshop offers a continuum of writing modules that takes a student from beginning to end. Whether the student has learning disabilities or not, the program is customizable and offers the educator the tools to differentiate instruction to benefit the learner. At the primary level, students are afforded an opportunity to draw and use inventive spelling to get their point across, while at the intermediate level, the expectation is for more formal writing to occur. Students learn the process through the mini-lesson, interactive/independent writing, and a sharing of work prior to publishing student pieces.

INSTRUCTIONAL APPROACHES TO STUDENTS WITH LEARNING DISABILITIES

Providing classroom accommodations and instructional practices allows students who struggle with writing to feel supported, and thus increases their motivation for writing. Classroom accommodations such as using graphic organizers, grouping larger assignments into smaller chunks, and giving students rubrics and exemplars of finished work are effective at supporting students with learning disabilities (Connelly et al., 2009; Morin, 2014; Troia, 2013).

In addition to accommodations, considerations for instructional approaches must be addressed. Setting clear goals for students provides a clear direction and offers initial guidance. The use of explicit teaching strategies is often needed when working with students with learning disabilities. Finally, providing structured and consistent time for daily writing is necessary for maintaining support, opportunities for practice, and individual student growth (Troia 2013; Troia and Olinghouse, 2013).

As if that were not enough, educators must provide encouragement and teach self-monitoring skills, and provide opportunities for students to collaborate in the drafting, planning, and revising processes. Finally, educators must model, explain, and scaffold instructions; set high expectations; implement the use of portfolios and rubrics; and assign grades that reflect growth over time (Troia 2013; Troia and Olinghouse, 2013). This long list of requirements will provide the necessary backdrop for struggling students and those with learning disabilities to become writers in their own right.

FINAL THOUGHTS

The Individuals with Disabilities Education Improvement Act of 2004 as well as the Every Student Succeeds Act mandate the use of evidence-based instructional strategies to close the achievement gap by ensuring the best possible teaching practices are in place for all students. Coupled with legislation, the Common Core State Standards underscore the importance of proficiency in written expression, thus encouraging and supporting the use of evidence-based teaching practices in the area of writing (Gilbert and Graham, 2010; Troia and Olinghouse, 2013).

For students with learning disabilities, the process of writing effectively and developing the skills necessary to do so can be frustrating and overwhelming, resulting in a lack of motivation to write. Learning disabilities can affect areas of written expression, including spelling accuracy, grammar and punctuation, handwriting, and organization and clarity of written expression (Connelly et al., 2009).

The writing process is a complex endeavor that incorporates several cognitive, linguistic, affective, and behavior skills (Troia and Olinghouse, 2013). The integration of this complex set of skills can be affected by impairments in both short- and long-term working memory, as evidenced in students with dyslexia, as these impairments directly affect the ability to successfully execute multiple cognitive tasks (Berninger et al., 2013).

There are promising evidence-based strategies for teaching writing skills. One practice, known as Self-Regulation Strategy Development (SRSD), has shown a positive impact in writing development for students with LD, students with ADHD, as well as students who simply struggle with writing (Harris and Graham, 2013). SRSD combines both explicit instruction along with supported independent practice.

Students with LD struggle tremendously with spelling and, therefore, explicit spelling instruction is a critical component to any writing curriculum (Harris et al., 2017). This student population need to be able to correctly and automatically spell common words that appear in primary and adolescent writing. Developing automaticity in spelling allows students with LD to devote more cognitive energy to the writing process itself.

The implementation of Writer's Workshops for students with LD and those who struggle with writing has proven to be positive as it focuses on the writing process as a whole and as individual skills as well as a community-building experience. Studies have indicated positive results in both writing gains and social interactions for students whose educators use the workshop model with fidelity (Gair, 2015; Troia, 2013; Wiley and McKernan, 2016).

POINTS TO REMEMBER

- *Research suggests that the most prevalent characteristics of writing weaknesses for students with learning disabilities pertain to spelling inaccuracies and deficits in writing fluency.*
- *Writing is a complex process involving cognitive, linguistic, affective, and behavioral skills working together. Students with one or more of these impairments may become easily frustrated with the writing process.*
- *Students with learning disabilities may experience additional difficulties in planning, organizing their thoughts, expressing their thoughts, spelling,*

and revising when writing, which then requires skill building, accommodations, and modifications in order to be successful writers.
- Evidence-based instructional practices are mandated in ESSA, a practice that began with IDEIA and continued with NCLB.
- The Common Core State Standards stress the importance of proficiency in written expression across all curricular domains, making differentiated writing instruction necessary.

The primary author can be reached at nyoung1191@aol.com.

REFERENCES

American Speech-Language-Hearing Association. (2017). *Specific Learning Disabilities*. Retrieved from https://www.asha.org/advocacy/federal/idea/04-law-specific-ld/

American Speech-Language-Hearing Association (n.d.). *Language-based learning disabilities (reading, spelling, and writing)*. Retrieved from http://www.asha.org/content.aspx?id=14069.

Archer, A., and Hughes, C. (2011). *Explicit instruction: Effective and efficient teaching*. New York: Guilford Press.

Bear, D., Invernizzi, M, Templeton, S., and Johnston, F. (2015). *Words their way*. 6th ed. Boston, MA: Pearson.

Berninger, V., Lee, Y., Abbott, R., and Breznitz, Z. (2013). Teaching children with dyslexia to spell in a reading-writer's workshop. *Annals of Dyslexia, 63*, 1–24. Retrieved from http://web.b.ebscohost.com.ezproxy.springfield.edu/ehost/pdfviewer/pdfviewer?vid=1&sid=9296cf73-30da-44b3-ae70-eb66ded2ca71%40sessionmgr104.

De La Paz, S., and Sherman, C. (2013). Revising strategy instruction in inclusive settings: Effects for English learners and novice writers. *Learning Disabilities Research and Practice, 28*(3), 129–41. Retrieved from http://web.b.ebscohost.com.ezproxy.springfield.edu/ehost/pdfviewer/pdfviewer?vid=1&sid=76586de8-081a-4c7e-84cd-6a18df233321%40sessionmgr103.

Dockrell, J. E., Lindsay, G., and Connelly, V. (2009). The Impact of Specific Language Impairment on Adolescents' Written Text. *Exceptional children, 15*, 427–446.

Ennis, R., Jolivette, K., Terry, N., Frederick, L. and Alberto, P. (2015). Classwide teacher implementation of self-regulated strategy development for writing with students with E/BD in a residential facility. *Journal of Behavioral Education, 24*, 88–111. Retrieved from http://web.a.ebscohost.com.ezproxy.springfield.edu/ehost/pdfviewer/pdfviewer?vid=1&sid=f35df6a1-6d00-4ff3-8e91-291de86838ab%40sessionmgr4006.

Flanagan, S., and Bouck, E. (2015). Mapping out the details: Supporting struggling writer's written expression with concept mapping. *Preventing School Failure, 59*(4), 244–52. Retrieved from http://web.a.ebscohost.com.ezproxy.springfield.edu/ehost/pdfviewer/pdfviewer?vid=1&sid=4513413b-0e67-4101-b9d3-e72b45b9acb7%40sessionmgr4009.

Gair, M. (2015). Slaying the writing monsters: Scaffolding reluctant writers through a writing workshop approach. *International Journal of Teaching and Learning in Higher Education, 27*(3), 443–56. Retrieved from http://files.eric.ed.gov/fulltext/EJ1093717.pdf.

Gilbert, J., and Graham, S. (2010). Teaching writing to elementary students in grades 4 to 6: A national survey. *Elementary School Journal, 110*, 494–518. Retrieved from http://www.journals.uchicago.edu.ezproxy.springfield.edu/doi/full/10.1086/651193.

Graham, S. (1999). Handwriting and spelling instruction for students with learning disabilities: A review. *Learning Disability Quarterly, 22*, 78-98.

Graham, S., Harris, K., and Chambers, A. (2016). Evidence-based practice and writing instruction. A review of reviews. In C. MacArthur, S. Graham, and J. Fitzgerald (eds.), *Handbook of writing research* (pp. 211–26). New York: Guilford Press.

Graham, S., and Santangelo, T. (2014). Does spelling instruction make students better spellers, readers, and writers? A meta-analytic review. *Reading and Writing: An Interdisciplinary Journal*, 27, 1703–43. Retrieved from https://eric.ed.gov/?id=EJ1041016.

Harris, K., and Graham, S. (2013). An adjective is a word hanging down from a noun: Learning to write and students with learning disabilities. *Annals of Dyslexia*, 63, 65–79. Retrieved from http://web.a.ebscohost.com.ezproxy.springfield.edu/ehost/pdfviewer/pdfviewer?vid=1&sid=8ccde063-dbaa-425e-a486-349a071ebd2d%40sessionmgr4006.

Harris, K., Graham, S., Aitken, A., Barkel, A., Houston, J., and Ray, A. (2017). Teaching spelling, writing, and reading for writing: Powerful evidence-based practices. *Teaching Exceptional Children*, 49(4), 262–72. Retrieved from http://journals.sagepub.com.ezproxy.springfield.edu/doi/pdf/10.1177/0040059917697250.

Individuals with Disabilities Education Improvement Act. (2004). 34 CFR§612.8(c)(10), 2004.

Johnson, E., Hancock, C., Carter, D., and Pool, J. (2012). Self-regulated strategy development as a tier 2 writing intervention. *Intervention in School and Clinic. Hamill Institute on Disabilities*, 48(4), 218–22. Retrieved from http://journals.sagepub.com.ezproxy.springfield.edu/doi/abs/10.1177/1053451212462880?journalCode=iscc&volume=48&year=2013&issue=4.

Mason, L., Harris, K., and Graham, S. (2011). Self-regulated strategy development for students with writing difficulties. The College of Education and Human Ecology. *Ohio State University: Theory into Practice*, 50(20), 20–27. Retrieved from http://web.a.ebscohost.com.ezproxy.springfield.edu/ehost/pdfviewer/pdfviewer?vid=1&sid=fdcd5c94-4443-46b3-ae1a-86368bbc909f%40sessionmgr4008.

Morin, A. (2014). At a glance: classroom accommodations for dysgraphia. *Understood for Learning and Attention Issues*. Retrieved from https://www.understood.org/en/school-learning/partnering-with-childs-school/instructional-strategies/at-a-glance-classroom-accommodations-for-dysgraphia.

Nation, K. (2011). Disorders of reading and writing. In P. C. Hogan (ed.), *The Cambridge encyclopedia of the language sciences* (pp. 267–69). New York: Cambridge University Press.

National Center for Education Statistics. (2012). The nation's report card: Writing 2011 (NECES 2012-470). Washington, DC: Institute of Educational Sciences, US Department of Education. Retrieved from https://nces.ed.gov/nationsreportcard/pdf/main2011/2012470.pdf.

Taft, R., and Mason, L. H. (2011). Examining effect of writing interventions: Highlighting results for students with primary disabilities other than learning disabilities. *Remedial and Special Education*, 32(5), 359–70. Retrieved from http://journals.sagepub.com/doi/10.1177/0741932510362242.

Troia, G. (2013). Writing instruction within a response-to-intervention framework. In S. Graham, C. MacArthur, and J. Fitzgerald (eds.), *Best practices in writing instruction*. 2nd ed. New York: Guilford.

Troia, G., and Olinghouse, N. (2013). The common core state standards and evidence-based educational practices: the case of writing. *School Psychology Review*, (42)3, 343–57. Retrieved from http://web.a.ebscohost.com.ezproxy.springfield.edu/ehost/pdfviewer/pdfviewer?vid=1&sid=3cae3fe0-9716-4115-9fd5-b00b03d2a12b%40sessionmgr4007.

Wiley, A., and McKernan, J. (2016). Examining the impact of explicit language instruction in writers workshop on ell student writing. *New Educator*, 13(2), 160–69. https://doi.org/10.1080/1547688X.2016.1144122.

Chapter Eight

Effective Home–School Partnerships

Strategies for Ensuring Collaboration for Families with Children with Learning Disabilities

Nicholas D. Young, *American International College*, and Elizabeth Jean, *Endicott College*

Home–school partnerships have the ability to make or break a student's academic career, and no connection is more important than that of a school to a family whose student has a learning disability. Bridging the two sides, home–school partnerships offer families a way to connect with their child and the environment in which he learns daily, while the educator has the chance to understand where the child comes from and who is important to them.

This two-way communication is the basis for a long, healthy relationship; however, sometimes this process needs to be coaxed or is nonexistent. In those cases, it is the responsibility of the school to work toward solutions that benefit the student. The effectiveness of educational partnerships, especially for students with disabilities, depends on how schools and families engage or partner with each other.

For many years, the terms *family involvement* and *family engagement* were interchangeable; however, they denote two very different manners for schools and families to come together in the educational process. Understanding the difference helps to create a best-case scenario for student success. To "involve" is defined as "to enfold or envelop" while to "engage" is defined as "to do or take part in something, to come together" (Merriam-Webster, 2017). The difference between the two, therefore, is that involvement suggests doing to while engagement entails doing with.

Connecting schools and families has been a tenet of both federal and state legislation since 1965 with Title I of the Elementary and Secondary Education Act (ESEA). In 2002, No Child Left Behind (NCLB) reenergized ESEA, and in 2015 Every Student Succeeds Act (ESSA) rewrote the family engagement portion to incorporate greater budgetary spending meant to directly involve parents and families, whether foster or natural, along with schools and educators (Duncan, 2015). Essentially, states and districts who took federal monies were bound by specific laws to include families.

The updated ESSA supported the strengthening of family engagement and tasked both educational leaders and families to take active roles in the process. ESSA laid out specific guidelines for families of and students with disabilities including a renewed call to ensure that barriers are reduced, appropriate accommodations and supports are in place, expectations are for high achievement, and, of course, two-way communication is encouraged (Henderson, 2016; Council of Chief State School Officers, 2016).

The expanded definition of family engagement rests on research showing how parents play significant roles in supporting their children's learning, not only in the home but also by guiding their children successfully through complex school systems and becoming vocal advocates for their children and for shared, effective public school experiences (Epstein, 2011; Flamboyan Classroom Family Engagement Rubric, 2011; Mapp and Kuttner, 2013).

Family engagement is not limited to helping children at home. Adults play a major role in determining whether their children take advantage of all the educational opportunities available to them; however, this cannot be accomplished without the cooperative efforts of educators—in this instance, special education teachers. Family engagement, therefore, is an important component to ensure collaboration between home and school or caregivers and educators for the purpose of increasing academic success for students.

Grant and Ray (2015) explain that family engagement requires "a mutually collaborative, working relationship with the family [that] serves the best interests of the student, in both school and home settings, for the primary purpose of increasing student achievement" (p. 6). It is incumbent on the school to provide ongoing and positive ways in which to engage with families. Nurturing relationships with families and giving them the tools to participate in their child's academic environment is necessary in order for there to be attainable success for students, especially those with special needs.

PARTNERSHIP MODELS

Although quite a bit of work has been done to educate parents on effective ways to engage with their children's schools and teachers, training educators to use effective strategies in engaging parents with schools has taken a back seat (Epstein, 2011). Within the last decade, however, several models have developed to assist educators, school leaders, and districts to partner with families to improve academic outcomes.

School-Family-Community Partnership Model

Joyce Epstein, one of the seminal experts on family-school partnerships, provided a comprehensive model to help parents become involved with schools and foster improved educational outcomes for their children. The six types or "keys" lay the groundwork for the partnership between family and school; and rather than explaining the "why" (i.e., theoretical framework), explain the "how" (i.e., partnerships) (Grant and Ray, 2015).

Epstein's (1987, 2011) work provided the keys for parental engagement in the educational process: parenting, communicating, volunteering, learning at home, decision-making, and collaborating with community. In this framework, educators made efforts to equip parents with the tools to help children develop academically when away from school. These parameters included training for parent programs and other services to support the well-being of families (Epstein, 1987, 2011).

The keys also offer suggestions of what results might look like for students, families, and teachers. Over time, Epstein expanded on her original work, which also gave opportunity to other scholars to develop ways in which family-school relationships could improve their partnerships (Epstein, 2011; Harvard Family Research Project, 2014; Mapp and Kuttner, 2013; Merrill, 2015).

Dual Capacity-Building Framework for Family-School Partnerships

Similar to Epstein's model, Mapp and Kuttner (2013) suggested a dual capacity-building framework for family-school partnerships. Endorsed by Arne Duncan, the dual capacity-building framework acts as a "compass . . . to chart a path toward effective family engagement efforts that are linked to student achievement and school improvement" (p. 6), not a "blueprint for engagement initiatives" (p. 6). There are four parts to the compass that are considered essential elements: challenge, opportunity conditions, policy and program goals, and, lastly, family and staff capacity outcomes.

Challenge refers to the lack of opportunity by families, staff, and school to build partnerships. *Opportunity conditions* is a broad term linked to process and organizational conditions. Process conditions refer to collaboration, interactivity, and linking knowledge to learning, while organizational conditions are tied to systemic change, integrated change in all programs, and sustained change using resources.

Within the *policy and program goals*, Mapp and Kuttner (2013) refer to the 4 Cs: capabilities (skills and knowledge), connections (networks), cognition (values and beliefs), and confidence (self-efficacy). Lastly, *family and staff capacity outcomes* are twofold. The school and staff are tasked with connecting family engagement to student learning, creating a welcoming school culture, and honoring family knowledge, while families are tasked with supporting, encouraging, advocating, and collaborating, which ultimately aid in student achievement and school culture (Mapp and Kuttner, 2013).

Other Models

The Harvard Family Research Project (2014) study reemphasized Epstein's original philosophy of family-school engagement as a way to further academic success of students. Students with special needs require in-depth support in many academic areas. These students need the "benefits of a complementary learning approach, in which an array of school and non-school supports complement one another to create an integrated set of community-wide resources that support learning and development from birth to young adulthood" (Harvard, 2014).

Community collaboration is yet another connection teachers and staff may use to meet families and build trusting, cooperative partnerships. Endorsed by the National Education Foundation (2012) and used in many states, the National Education Association (NEA) has provided assistance to form solid bonds with families.

In Springfield, Massachusetts, the Springfield Collaborative for Change (SCC) in conjunction with the NEA has provided techniques for collaboration between school and home. Regardless of the partnership model, research indicates that parents have an influential role in the development of their children's academic achievement from birth to adulthood (Epstein, 2011; Hynes, 2014).

In early childhood, parents play a major role in the development of children's cognitive and language skills. During the middle and high school years, parents help their children by fostering educational socialization and helping them prepare for future college and career achievement, which in totality enhances the idea of family engagement throughout a child's academic career (Hynes, 2014). For these important reasons, it is necessary for schools and educators to engage in strategies that provide opportunities for partnership with families to increase the academic success of students with disabilities.

STRATEGIES FOR ENSURING COLLABORATION

Not only is there a variety of home–school partnership models, there is also a plethora of strategies that can be used to gain and maintain a high level of engagement between school and the family of a student with a disability. The strategies, when used correctly, provide a level of comfort and connection, increasing the odds for student achievement.

Included in the list of strategies are cultural considerations, inclusion of community members, as well as helping families understand and come to terms with a disability. The best home–school partnerships, however, have developed an uncompromised level of communication that has been carefully cultivated, thus making the team effective in providing just-right services for the student with disabilities.

Cultural Considerations

Special education programs and educators should attempt to learn about the families for whom they work, especially the culture of their families. Understanding cultural ideas about diet, health, and other basic family data allows the school community to provide appropriate services to fulfill the needs of students (Hutchins, Greenfield, Epstein, Sanders, and Galindo, 2012; Quinton, 2013).

Though families may retain their cultural backgrounds and experiences, school enhances cultural exchanges that may separate generations within a family, often creating a better understanding between home and school as families grapple with the new cultural and social experiences of their children (Hutchins, Greenfield, Epstein, Sanders, and Galindo, 2012; Grant and Ray, 2015).

According to Camarota (2015), the 2014 American Community Survey shows that 21 percent of US residents speak a language other than English when at home. Being mindful of these growing linguistic differences, school administrators and educators will want to ensure translation services for calls home, conferences, team meetings, assessments, and Individual Education Plan (IEP) meetings. Additionally, it is important that all paperwork, newsletters, and messages are sent home in the native language.

Some schools may have limited translation services available in house, such as a Spanish-speaking teacher; however, at times it is necessary to hire out services. Gould, the founder of the translation company thebigword, explains that "language localisation" (2017, n.p.) is important to break down barriers, and although he is discussing the business world, the same can be said for education. Additionally, apps such as ClassDojo (ClassDojo, 2017) can translate messages into over thirty languages, allowing communication between educator and family at the touch of a button on any laptop or smart device, encouraging dialogue and connection.

Including Community Members

The values, attitudes, and beliefs of parents regarding education have a direct impact on student academic performance (Harvard, 2014; Mapp and Kuttner, 2013). Schools cannot adequately address the needs of their special education students without contributions from their families. Redefining family engagement means creating integrated community-wide programs and/or connecting with outside agencies to help children succeed.

Sanders (2014) reports that 13 percent of America's K–12 students have "identified disabilities." Knowing this, it is vital that schools collaborate with families and agencies, or individuals, to make sense of the disability and provide necessary services both in and outside of school (Stefanski, Valli, and Jacobson, 2016). All stakeholders must be thoughtful as to how best to help the student who may have social, behavioral, and/or academic considerations while ensuring that those services are "purposeful, relevant, and timely" (Sanders, 2014).

Understanding the Process

An educator usually has a sixth sense about a student who just isn't catching on to grade-level material. Classroom assessments, both formative and summative, will confirm this. A parent may notice that something just isn't right—they may not know exactly what it is, but their child may not be growing, either physically or mentally, like others around him. At these times, it is important to bring the concerns to the table in a parent/educator meeting (National Center for Learning Disabilities, 2017). It is the duty of both sides to present the facts, not the emotions, and make decisions to best help the child.

At this meeting, the team may decide to first try a six- to eight-week intensive intervention; many schools use a Response to Intervention (RTI) model (National Center for Learning Disabilities, 2017). The team, consisting of family and educators, then comes back together: Did the intervention work and should it be continued? Does the intervention need to be tweaked and tried again? Or, is a period of assessment warranted? At each step, it is important to include family and explain the options as well as listening to the family's concerns, taking all viewpoints into consideration (Learning Disabilities of America, 2017).

Should it be decided that an evaluation referral is necessary, the team leader should explain the process to the parent; giving a linguistically appropriate fact sheet helps the family understand. Massachusetts, in conjunction with the Federation for Children with Special Needs (2017), offers a pamphlet in several languages that explains the entire process. The referral, assessment, and eligibility process can be confusing; thus, the more information that can be front-loaded to the family, the better. Directing families to an organization or state website that explains the process can be helpful.

The Center for Parent Information and Resources (2017) and Learning Disabilities Worldwide (2017) both maintain websites replete with articles and helpful tools parents can access to help them understand the process. Rhode Island, for example, has developed a website that offers families a comprehensive look into the world of special education, offering information on regulations, resources, programming options, the IEP process, and much more (Rebhorn, 2017).

Once the evaluation process has been completed, the team will meet to go over the testing results. It is helpful to send home the report in advance so that the family can read it over and gather questions. During the meeting, it will be vital for all educators and testers to explain each individual test, its purpose, and the outcomes in a family-friendly manner (Eichenstein, 2015).

Refrain from using jargon and acronyms that may not be familiar to the family; allow for questions and discussion (Eichenstein, 2015). It may be necessary for the tester to remind the family to go home, read the results again, digest, and later ask questions—the family must feel comfortable and be part of the process in order for positive results to occur (Eichenstein, 2015).

Should an IEP be determined as necessary, it will be created with input from all stakeholders. If the student is deemed ineligible for an IEP, the team might feel a 504 is necessary (Lee, 2017). This federally mandated document has its own set of requirements and allows for student accommodations in a variety of settings based on medical need. In either case, yearly meetings review progress, make new goals, and update accommodations. Although having and IEP or 504 in place is necessary for the student with disabilities, helping families come to terms with the disability can be a difficult but important step (Lee, 2017).

Helping Families Come to Terms with the Disability

Educators deal with student learning disabilities all the time, making accommodations and talking to families is commonplace; however, the student is not their child and as such, the emotional aspect is rarely addressed. A parent, however, hears this news—their child has a learning disability—and their mind shuts down (Eichenstein, 2015). They may not hear what the team is saying or understand what it means. For them, having an atypical child was not part of the plan and they will need help to come to a place of understanding and acceptance.

According to Eichenstein (2015), there are five stages of acceptance: denial, anger and blame, bargaining and seeking solutions, depression, and active acceptance. Each stage produces a flood of differing emotions that the parent must deal with; having the school to count on is important. The parent may need to lean on the teacher, the counselor, or the team leader at different times. It may be important to find outside help for the family. Each situation is different; effective administrator/educator teams must bridge the gap, be good listeners, and offer guidance and sage advice when asked or when needed.

Communication and Shared Responsibility

Educator communication to family members is just one component of shared responsibility, as it addresses ways in which contributions may be made to student educational success. Mutually agreed-upon roles for family members and schools become a hallmark of shared responsibility, as it is more than just asking parents to participate (Epstein, 2011; Mapp and Kuttner, 2013). Additionally, regardless of resources, shared responsibility suggests that every family can do something to help a student achieve academic success with the caveat that, although this is possible, the willingness of both parties must be considered; thus, inhibiting the contributions made (Hynes, 2014).

Using communication as a strategy, educators must often move out of their comfort zone and make an extra effort to connect with families. Being a good communicator takes on a variety of meanings. Providing journals with daily entries and points sheets are good starting points, but it may be better to call home and/or invite the parent in regularly. It may be that the educator connects with families via email or text, or uses the ClassDojo (2017) as the primary form of communication sending pictures and messages.

Barriers exist when families are intimidated or do not feel comfortable with an educational professional; thus, it is important for the educator to find the best communication method possible and use that to his or her advantage (Family Empowerment and Disability Council, 2012).

Home Visit Programs

A discussion on home–school partnerships for students with learning disabilities would not be complete without a discussion regarding home visits. A home-visit program can be a catalyst for change and collaboration. This valuable task provides a familiar place for families to learn about the school, class, teacher, or specific program their child will be involved with. Additionally, families may be more open to hearing about the learning disability of their student when on home turf.

Prior to visiting the home, it is imperative to make an appointment and state the reason for the visit—for example, to explain the IEP process, to describe the program, to talk about student progress (Grant and Ray, 2015). All stakeholders should attend—the counselor, educator, and team leader and/or a translator if necessary. It will be important to include the student in the visit. To ensure buy-in from the family and student, educational professionals must essentially sell themselves and the program.

The Parent/Teacher Home Visit Project (PTHVP) of Sacramento, California, endorsed by the National Education Association (NEA), has been touted as an "investment in teacher effectiveness and enriched student learning" because the families, students, and teachers "come together through home visits to change educational outcomes for the better" (NEA, 2012, p. 2). This program suggests a series of visits throughout the year and over the whole of the student's academic career and is based on a co-educator approach where the parent is half of the collaboration equation. In this way, a student with disabilities and their family can feel comfortable and reassured that the staff has the student's best interest in mind.

FINAL THOUGHTS

Partnering with families to create better outcomes for students with learning disabilities takes on many forms, from ensuring they understand the process to sourcing out services, from helping families through the emotions related to diagnosis to guiding them through difficult conversations. Families need assistance to understand the process and make informed decisions that will impact the education of their child. It is the job of the school and educator to ensure a successful partnership.

Open communication and home visits may help bridge gaps in the comfort level of families while bringing families into school allows them to see where the student works and what the expectations are. One thing is certain: when aiming for a solid home–school partnership, collaboration is key and communication is essential.

POINTS TO REMEMBER

- *Home–school partnerships are, by nature, a coming together of persons in order to ensure the success of a student—in this case, a student with a learning disability.*
- *The Every Student Succeeds Act supports and requires collaboration between educational professionals and families of students with learning disabilities using specific guidelines.*

- *A variety of partnership models exists—the common thread is that they all value collaboration and communication between home and school.*
- *Cultural considerations include translation services as needed to improve communication with linguistically diverse populations.*
- *Community members should be included in meetings and services should be suggested when it is in the student's best interest.*
- *Families must understand the referral, assessment, and eligibility process but it is up to the educational professionals to provide this information in a way that is easy for families to understand.*
- *Home visits are another tool to engage with reticent families and build comfortable connections that lead to positive school outcomes for students with learning disabilities.*

The primary author can be reached at nyoung1191@aol.com.

REFERENCES

Camarota, S. (2015). Immigration worked out fine in the past, so relax, say authors of an influential new study. Retrieved from http://www.nationalreview.com/article/427913/flawed-one-sided-study-immigrant-assimilation-steven-camarota.

Center for Parent Information and Resources. (2017). *Supporting the parent centers who serve families of children with disabilities*. Retrieved from http://www.parentcenterhub.org/.

Class DoJo (2017). *Introducing: ClassDojo translate*. Retrieved from https://blog.classdojo.com/introducing-classdojo-translate/.

Council of Chief State School Officers. (2016). *ESSA: Key provisions and implications for students with disabilities*. Retrieved from http://www.ccsso.org/resources/programs/Every_Student_Succeeds_Act.html.

Duncan, A. (2015). *ESEA Speech to Congress*. Retrieved from http://www.ed.gov/blog/2015/01/opportunity-is-not-optional-secretary-duncans-vision-for-americas-landmark-education-law/.

Eichenstein, R. (2015). *Not what I expected: Help and hope for parents of atypical children*. New York: Penguin.

Epstein, J. L. (2011). *School, family, and community partnerships: Preparing educators and improving schools* (2nd ed.). Boulder, CO: Westview Press.

Epstein, J. L. (1987). *Toward a theory of family-school connections: Teacher practices and parent involvement across the school years*. In K. Hurrelmann, F. Kaufmann, and F. Losel (Eds.), *Social Intervention: Potential and constraints*, 121–136. New York, NY: de Gruyter.

Federation for Children with Special Needs. (2017). *A parent's guide to special education*. Retrieved from http://fcsn.org/parents-guide.

Flamboyan Classroom Family Engagement Rubric (2011). *Flamboyan Institute*. Washington D.C. and Puerto Rico. Retrieved from http://www.roadmapproject.org/wp-content/uploads/2012/11/Final-Report_Engaged-Parents-Successful-Students-Report-9-12-12.pdf.

Gould, L. (2017). *Forget Spanglish—Why it's vital to communicate with customers in their own language*. Retrieved from https://en-us.thebigword.com/news/forget-spanglish-why-it-s-vital-to-communicate-with-customers-in-their-own-language.

Grant, K. B., and Ray, J. A. (2015). *Home, school, and community collaboration: Culturally responsive family engagement*. 3rd ed. Thousand Oaks, CA: Sage.

Harvard Family Research Project. (2014). *Redefining family engagement for student success*. Retrieved from http://www.hfrp.org/redefining-family-engagement-for-student-success.

Henderson, A. T. (2016). *Quick brief on family engagement in Every Child Succeeds Act (ESSA) of 2015.* Retrieved from https://ra.nea.org/wp-content/uploads/2016/06/FCE-in-ESSA-in-Brief.pdf.

Hutchins, D. J., Greenfield, M. D., Epstein, J. L., Sanders, M. G., and Galindo, C. (2012). *Multicultural partnerships involve all families.* New York: Routledge.

Hynes, W. (2014). Meet the family: Teaching tolerance. Retrieved from http://www.tolerance.org/sites/default/files/general/Meet%20the%20Family.pdf.

Learning Disabilities of America. (2017). *The role of parents/families in RTI.* Retrieved from https://ldaamerica.org/the-role-of-parentsfamily-in-response-to-intervention/?doing_wp_cron=1499880386.1829659938812255859375.

Learning Disabilities Worldwide. (2017). *Parents.* Retrieved from https://www.ldworldwide.org/parents.

Lee, A. M. (2017). *The difference between IEPs and 504 plans.* Retrieved from https://www.understood.org/en/school-learning/special-services/504-plan/the-difference-between-ieps-and-504-plans.

Mapp, K. L., and Kuttner, P. J. (2013). *Partners in education: A dual capacity-building framework for family-school partnerships.* Retrieved from http://www.ed.gov/parent-and-family-engagement.

Merriam-Webster. (2017). s.v. "involve." Retrieved from https://www.merriam-webster.com/dictionary/involve.

Merriam-Webster. (2017). s.v. "engage." Retrieved from https://www.merriam-webster.com/dictionary/engage.

Merrill, S. (2015). Head start and the evolving concept of family involvement. *Head Start.* Retrieved from http://eclkc.ohs.acf.hhs.gov/hslc/hs/news/blog/define-involvement.html.

National Center for Learning Disabilities. (2017). *What is RTI?* Retrieved from http://www.rtinetwork.org/learn/what/whatisrti.

National Education Association. (2012). *Parent/teacher home visit: Creating a bridge between parents and teachers as co-educators in Springfield, MA and Seattle, WA. NEA Foundation Issue Brief.* Retrieved from http://www.neafoundation.org/content/assets/2012/03/pthv-full-issue-brief-5.pdf.

Quinton, S. (2013). Good teachers embrace their students' cultural backgrounds. *Atlantic.* Retrieved from https://www.theatlantic.com/education/archive/2013/11/good-teachers-embrace-their-students-cultural-backgrounds/281337/.

Rebhorn, T. (2017). Developing your child's IEP. Retrieved from www.parentcenterhub.org.

Rhode Island Department of Education. *Special Education.* Retrieved from http://www.ride.ri.gov/StudentsFamilies/SpecialEducation.aspx.

Sanders, M. G. (2014). *It takes a village: School-community collaboration.* Retrieved from http://www.calstat.org/publications/article_detail.php?a_id=216&nl_id=131.

Stefanski, A., Valli, L., and Jacobson, R. (2016). *Beyond involvement and engagement: The role of family in school-community partnerships.* Retrieved from http://www.schoolcommunitynetwork.org/SCJ.aspx.

US Department of Education. (2002). No Child Left Behind: Parental involvement: Title I. Retrieved from www2.ed.gov/nclb/landing.jhtml.

Chapter Nine

Effective Behaviors Employed by Successful Teachers of Students with Learning and Emotional Challenges

A Framework for Better Teaching

Vance L. Austin, *Manhattanville College*

All teacher candidates must now acquire the skills and dispositions necessary to teach students with learning and emotional challenges. Teacher preparation courses must find ways to ensure that teacher candidates are prepared to "reach and teach" this emotionally tenuous population. As one step in the reflective process of teacher preparation practices, the effective behaviors of successful teachers need to be considered. To remain relevant, teacher preparation programs must begin to study the qualities that effective teachers of students with learning and emotional and behavioral disorders demonstrate and which of the identified qualities can be taught to teacher candidates.

One framework that is beneficial to the process is Kennedy's (2008), in which he classifies effective teacher behaviors according to one of three categories: (a) personal resources, the qualities that the teacher brings to the job; (b) teacher performance, teachers' everyday practices that occur in and out of the classroom; and (c) teacher effectiveness, the relational teacher qualities that influence students. This chapter will provide a framework based on the author's original research, enhanced by current "best practices" in the field, such as Kennedy's (2008), that teachers can use to improve their effectiveness relative to this delicate population.

The teaching model known as inclusion requires the collaboration of both special and general educators and the ability to accommodate and provide services for diverse classroom populations. As the inclusive classroom continues to develop into standard practice throughout the United States, classroom teachers can no longer claim students with special needs are not their responsibilities. Frequently, within the inclusion model, special and general educators are paired to serve students with a variety of needs in a single classroom. As a result, the role of the general education classroom teacher has changed.

All teacher candidates must now acquire the skills and dispositions necessary to teach students with a wide variety of needs. Teacher preparation courses must find ways to ensure that teacher candidates are prepared to teach such a diverse population in the inclusion model. As one step in the reflective process of teacher preparation practices, the pedagogical behaviors of successful teachers need to be considered. One group of students that are of great concern to teacher candidates are those individuals classified with learning and emotional/behavioral disorders.

School districts across the country have reported an increased number of students classified with emotional and behavioral disorders and concomitant learning challenges (Office of Special Education Programs, 2006). To remain current, teacher preparation programs must begin to evaluate the qualities that effective teachers of students with learning and emotional and behavioral disorders demonstrate and which of the identified qualities can be taught to teacher candidates. The concepts of effective teaching behaviors and teacher quality have proven elusive and difficult to define, so much so that the terms are frequently rendered useless (Kennedy, 2008).

PERSONAL RESOURCES

Kennedy (2008) described traits such as beliefs, attitudes, values, knowledge, skill, and expertise to be personal resources. Four basic personal qualities were repeatedly found in the research to be considered effective: knowledge of the subject area, respect for students, reflection on one's teaching, and taking an active role in one's professional growth.

Effective teachers are defined in the literature as highly qualified teachers who possess a passion for and strong knowledge base in their content area (Helm, 2007; Mowrer-Reynolds, 2008; Polk, 2006). Stough and Palmer (2003) reported that knowledge of special education instruction and the needs of each student are a central tenet of effective teaching.

Teachers who are effective believe in the potential of all children to learn. This belief is translated through the demonstration of respect for students (Mowrer-Reynolds, 2008), their families (Woolfolk, 2004), and student differences (Imber, 2006). Similarly, dispositions of caring, concern for children, and empathy are characteristics that should be hallmarks of effective teachers (Helm, 2007; Imber, 2006). For example, in one investigation, elementary students preferred teachers who showed that they truly cared for their well-being (Pratt, 2008).

Similarly, teaching efficacy is linked to a willingness to continuously develop as a professional (Harris, 1998). Helterbran (2008) noted that students defined good teachers as ones who are never satisfied with their teaching and are always eager to stretch, grow, and refine their teaching skills and subject knowledge. To remain effective, teachers must seek professional development opportunities and pursue lifelong learning (de Vries, Jansen, Helms-Lorenz, and van de Grift, 2015; Polk, 2006).

As both Harris (1998) and Larrivee (2000) have noted, the avenue to continued professional development is self-reflection and inquiry. Likewise, Topping and Ferguson (2005) recommended that all teachers should "have access to opportunities to monitor and reflect upon teaching behaviors they use and do not use, in different contexts" to enhance their teaching efficacy (p. 141).

In a study conducted by Stough and Palmer (2003) on the topic of special education instruction, the act of reflection and "concerned responsiveness of teacher to individual students" were central to effective teaching (p. 220). The challenge is to develop a system that enables teachers to transfer these newly acquired behaviors to the classroom so that the quality of teaching and student behavior can be improved (Bracey, 2009).

Teacher Performance

Performance qualities are teacher practices that occur daily such as providing optimal learning activities, employing techniques that facilitate student learning, and exploring ways to motivate or "entice" students to want to learn (Kennedy, 2008). For learning to take place, students need a safe and stimulating learning environment maintained through efficient classroom management (van de Grift, 2007). One important component of classroom management is clear communication.

Effective teaching is highly dependent on the teacher's ability to effectively communicate the instructional objectives (Harris, 1998; Polk, 2006; Sutherland, Lewis-Palmer, Stichter, and Morgan, 2008; van de Grift, 2007). Other qualities identified as characteristics of effective teachers include recognizing and using "teachable moments" (Woolfolk, 2004) and modeling new concepts and skills to ensure they are contextually understood (Polk, 2006).

Highlighted in the research is the necessity for flexibility in teaching methodology. Teachers need a repertoire of more than one pedagogical approach to be maximally effective in their teaching (Harris, 1998). Furthermore, effective teachers exercise creativity in adapting their teaching and their use of teaching-learning strategies to match the needs of different students (Rosenfeld and Rosenfeld, 2004; van de Grift, 2007; Woolfolk, 2004). Additionally, Rosenfeld and Rosenfeld (2004) reported sensitivity to individual learning differences as an integral component of effective teaching when working with students with special needs.

Teacher Effectiveness

Teacher qualities that influence students are labeled as effective (Kennedy, 2008). One way that effectiveness can be identified is by questioning students. Pratt (2008) and Biddulph and Adey (2004) studied the topic of teacher efficacy from the perspective of the student. Biddulph and Adey (2004) found that it was not the content of the curriculum that piqued students' interest in a subject, but rather it was the quality of the teaching and meaningfulness of the learning activities that influenced students' opinions about a teacher and the subject area.

Pratt (2008) noted that elementary-level students preferred teachers who made them feel like they were an important member of a community, provided choices in learning activities, allowed for cooperative projects, made learning seem fun, and used authentic and meaningful assessments. Other researchers also reported qualities related to humor as effective traits of teachers. For instance, Mowrer-Reynolds (2008) found teachers who were humorous, funny, and entertaining to be ranked highly as exemplary teacher characteristics. In addition to being humorous, teachers who were easy to talk to, were approachable, and provided outside help often were considered exemplary (Mowrer-Reynolds, 2008).

EFFECTIVE TEACHER PRACTICES RELATIVE TO SOCIAL AND ACADEMIC LEARNING

An area not addressed by Kennedy's framework, but clearly important to preservice and novice teachers, are research-based practices that have demonstrated efficacy in improving both academic and social performance for students. Some of the more promising of these include ensuring that instruction is both meaningful and engaging (Allen, Gregory, Mikami, Lun, Hamre, and Pianta, 2013; Gourneau, 2005; Scott, Hirn, and Alter, 2014), conscientiously improving classroom climate (Scott, Park, Swain-Bradway, and Landers, 2007), and the use of classwide peer tutoring (CWPT) to improve the academic performance of students with learning and emotional/behavioral needs (Hughes and Fredrick, 2006).

Still others comprise adventure therapy, a program that helps to build positive self-esteem and social skills (Dobud, 2016), teacher immediacy, the use of mnemonic devices and aids to help improve information storage and retrieval (Scruggs and Mastropieri, 2000), the teaching of cognitive behavioral (CBT) interventions such as "self-monitoring" (Hager, 2012; Patton, Jolivette, and Ramsey, 2006), and social emotional learning (SEL) techniques, such as "mindfulness" to reduce anxiety and increase focus and awareness (Jennings and Greenberg, 2009; Malow and Austin, 2016).

Additionally, the implementation of a positive behavioral support (PBS) system in the school and classroom to facilitate the inclusion of students with learning and emotional/behavioral challenges and effective inclusive practices to include collaborative or team teaching are also highly recommended best practices (Scott, Park, et al., 2007; Austin, 2001; Scanlon and Baker, 2012).

A positive correlation exists between teacher immediacy behaviors, attending to student needs in the moment, and concomitant student motivation and learning (Christophel, 1990; Crump, 1996). Similarly, Jennings and Greenberg (2009) investigated the impact of teachers' social and emotional competence (SEC) and well-being on the establishment of healthy, prosocial teacher-student relationships and its impact on classroom climate. As anticipated, they found a very positive and direct correlation between these elements.

In another study examining the qualities that students considered important in an effective teacher, the researcher noted the primacy of several: the ability to show empathy, the teacher's friendliness, the ability to communicate well with students, effective classroom management skills, and the provision of interesting and engaging lessons (Koutsoulis, 2003).

In a comparable investigation, Allen et al. (2013) observed that three teacher behaviors accounted for higher academic achievement on standardized achievement tests—namely, (a) a teacher-inspired positive emotional climate, (b) the use of various engaging instructional approaches, and (c) the teacher's focus on analysis and problem solving.

Finally, in another related study, Gourneau (2005) identified and examined five frequently acknowledged characteristics of effective classroom teachers. These five highly valued behaviors include: (a) a genuine, caring, and kind attitude toward students, (b) a willingness to delegate responsibility in the classroom and collaborate with others, (c) a keen awareness and celebration of student diversity, (d) the provision of meaningful learning experiences, and (5) a commitment to fostering and supporting students' creativity.

A review of the literature pertaining to teacher qualities and the efficacy of instruction revealed that most of the studies were conducted with general education teachers. Studies investigating the teacher qualities considered effective when teaching students with learning challenges and emotional and behavioral disorders specifically were few.

Research and experience both support the contention that teaching students classified as emotionally disturbed (ED) with concomitant learning problems present one of the greatest challenges for novice and inexperienced teachers and play a significant role in new teacher attrition (Billingsley, 2003; Nelson, Maculan, Roberts, and Ohlund, 2001; Singh and Billingsley, 1998). Despite the challenges posed by students with learning and behavioral problems, many experienced teachers have anecdotally reported consistent success in working with them.

Any initiative aimed at improving teacher success with these students should begin with an investigation of the effective practices employed by experienced, successful teachers.

The objectives of the author's investigation were to examine the effective teaching behaviors of highly qualified teacher-participants and to identify the behaviors that can be taught to teacher candidates.

For the purposes of the study, highly qualified teachers were defined as those with at least ten years of experience in working with students with learning and emotional and behavioral disorders, and who were confirmed by colleagues and the school's principal as effective practitioners who have had a record of superior standardized test scores achieved by their students. Employing this definition, four teachers (two males, two females) certified in special education, each with a minimum of ten years' teaching experience with students with emotional and behavioral disorders (EBD) were identified and participated in the study.

The four participants teach grades 10–12 in a private school located in the greater New York City area for students with EBD. Additionally, students defined as EBD were students who had gone through the New York State special education identification process and had been appropriately classified as such. Accordingly, twenty-one students from the school, all with an EBD classification and taught by the participating teachers, volunteered to complete a survey. Although students possessing an EBD classification vary in diagnosed disability, the student participants were identified as having demonstrated either externalizing behaviors, such as those evidenced in conduct disorders or ADHD, or internalizing behaviors, such as mood and anxiety disorders.

Three instruments adapted from previous studies were utilized in this investigation for data-collection purposes. First, an assessment of each teacher-participant's videotaped lesson was evaluated by means of a five-point Likert-type scale using the Checklist of Optimal Teaching Behaviors. This scale was based on the previous work of Harris (1998) and rated teaching behaviors on: (a) Analytic/Synthetic Approach, (b) Organization/Clarity, (c) Instructor Group Interaction, (d) Instructor-Individual Student Interaction, and (e) Dynamism/Enthusiasm.

Next, a semistructured interview, Interview Script for Teacher-Participants adapted from prior work of Cox (1996), was used to collect teacher-participants' perceptions of their pedagogy. This interview was tape-recorded and used a semistructured format. One of the four researchers conducted each teacher interview. The final instrument was a student participant survey, What Makes a Teacher Good?, developed to assess students' perceptions of teacher effectiveness.

The student survey provided the students with a list of some qualities that previous research has suggested are possessed by good teachers. Students were asked to select those qualities they felt were important for teachers to have and those qualities they felt their teacher possessed as the criteria for evaluating the teacher-participants. The survey employed a five-point Likert-type scale on the importance of specific teacher qualities and/or behaviors. Some background information about the student participant, such as age, grade level, and school experience, was also included.

Imber (2006) suggested that the principal way to determine the presence of effective teaching traits in a teacher is through observation of the teacher's classroom performance. To capture the teacher-participants' lesson for later coding, a fixed position video camera was in each classroom during which separate lessons were presented by the four participating teachers. The cameras were positioned prior to the entrance of the students into the classroom and remained unattended during the lesson. This unattended videotaping was done to avoid any added distraction from the lesson by an additional and novel adult in the classroom.

The cameras remained on for fifty minutes, the entirety of each class session. Two nonconsecutive instructional class periods were videotaped within a two-week period. Teacher-participants were instructed to carry out their planned lesson and interact with students present as they would normally do during a teaching session. After the lesson completion, the four researchers evaluated the teacher behaviors observed in each videotaped lesson. Each researcher individually evaluated all lessons and coded their responses to the videotape on the Checklist of Optimal Teaching Behaviors Likert-type scale, according to the protocol outlined by Harris (1998).

After the video analysis, one of the four researchers interviewed each teacher-participant. The purpose of these interviews was to assess participant perceptions of their own lesson and what they believed constituted effective pedagogy and positive teacher-student interaction. Participants responded to a semistructured script adapted from work previously conducted by Cox (1996). Each interview was tape-recorded and took place in the teacher-participants' classroom during a fifty-minute period.

For the final component, students in the teacher-participants' classrooms were asked to volunteer to complete a survey, What Makes a Good Teacher?, developed from criteria identified in prior investigations of teacher quality (Biddulph and Adey, 2004; Pratt, 2008). Students who agreed to participate completed the surveys at the beginning of assigned class time within a fifteen-minute time limit under supervision of the assistant teacher. Codes were placed on student surveys according to the teacher observed but were anonymous regarding student identification.

ANALYSIS OF DATA

The videotapes of the classroom practices and teaching behaviors of each of the teacher-participants were analyzed individually by each researcher. Subsequently, the team met to compare their perceptions of the teacher behaviors evident in the videotapes relative to each of the four teacher-participants. A consensus decision was achieved relative to each of the behaviors identified in the checklist that was used by all four investigators. Additional comments recorded individually by the researchers for each of the four teacher-participants were carefully analyzed to establish consensus.

In a similar manner, the interview transcripts of the responses of the teacher-participants were studied, first by each investigator and then communally, to identify and code both shared and unique teacher perceptions. Individual teacher responses were compared with their actual teaching behaviors as observed on the videotapes. Finally, all three data sets were cross-referenced to identify consistent findings.

RESULTS

After reviewing the three data sources (video, interview, and student survey), observations and responses were classified according to Kennedy's (2008) framework of effective teaching behaviors. The framework categorized effective behaviors into one of three components: (a) personal resources, (b) teacher performance, and (c) teacher effectiveness. Qualitative categories, examples, and percentages of student responses were recorded in tables. Additionally, a one-tailed Spearman Rank Correlation coefficient was conducted on the student survey responses (rho = .65, $p < .01$, $N = 14$).

The mean scores of identified effective teaching behaviors and the mean scores of the observed behaviors of the teachers, as determined by the researchers, were highly correlated. Thus, students equated the ideal qualities of effective teachers to be like the qualities that they observed in their own highly qualified experienced teachers.

DISCUSSION

The research objectives of the present investigation were to examine the effective teaching behaviors of highly qualified teacher-participants of students with EBD and to identify those behaviors deemed teachable for future inclusion in teacher preparation programs. During the research, the behaviors of four highly qualified teachers were observed. After analyzing the data from the videotapes, interviews, and student surveys, the researchers identified effective teaching behaviors.

The importance of Kennedy's (2008) framework for breaking effective teaching behaviors into teachable components for general educators was supported and was demonstrated to be applicable to teachers of students with EBD. Specifically, the effective behaviors of highly qualified experienced teachers of students with EBD fell within the three categories framed by Kennedy (2008) for general education teachers. The performance category presents teachable instructional and interpersonal behaviors. These included strategies such as awareness of body language, flexibility in accommodating different learning styles, active listening techniques, the use of eye contact, teacher availability, and incorporating a variety of teaching methodologies.

Goldhaber and Hansen (2017) indicated that while teacher certification procedures seek to identify effective teachers, in fact they might eliminate other teachers who may be proficient educators in the classroom. Effective teaching behaviors are not universal. Teachers need to know themselves and know their students to perform successfully in each situation. Although the identified qualities provide a guide for effective behaviors, teachers must seek to fit these behaviors into their own style.

Teacher preparation programs can utilize the qualities and behaviors identified to enhance instructional skills for teachers working with students with EBD. It is encouraging to discover that highly qualified teachers believe that many of the skills they possess can be successfully conveyed to those with less experience.

With the increase of the population of students with EBD (Office of Special Education Programs, 2006), particularly in the inclusive classroom, the awareness of these skills is relevant for both general education and special education teachers. The presentation of such teachable behaviors is essential to all teacher education programs.

FINAL THOUGHTS

As stated at the outset, the research objectives were to examine the effective teaching behaviors of highly qualified teacher-participants and to identify the behaviors that can be taught to teacher candidates. During the investigation, the examiners carefully analyzed the behaviors of four highly qualified teachers of students with emotional and behavioral disorders and were able to reach a consensus regarding those observed behaviors that they identified as effective and that were corroborated by the teachers themselves in one-to-one interviews. The outcomes from observed behaviors and teacher interviews were compared with the survey responses of some of the teacher-participants' students.

The implications of the findings of this preliminary investigation were limited by time constraints and the composition and small size of the participant sample; however, the author and his colleagues assert that they have modestly contributed to the identification of effective teacher behaviors that can be acquired through education and practice. The importance of the following teacher behaviors for educators who wish to be effective in teaching students with emotional and behavioral disorders were confirmed through this study.

Specifically, it was noted that educators need to: (a) explain clearly, (b) be well prepared, (c) provide lessons that are multimodal, (d) invite students to share their knowledge and experience, (e) demonstrate effective classroom management, (f) have a genuine interest in students, (g) be friendly toward students, (h) be enthusiastic about the subject, (i) possess self-confidence, and (k) have a sense of humor.

Teacher preparation faculty and professional development administrators, consequently, might consider ways to introduce these skills or to ensure they are clearly and comprehensively addressed in programs designed to prepare candidates to work with students with disabilities, such as those with learning and emotional/behavioral problems. Similarly, school administrators might use the qualities and behaviors recommended in this study as a "checklist" during the interview process to enhance their selection of the most qualified candidates for teaching positions that entail working with students with disabilities that include EBD.

Nevertheless, an appreciation of the value of these behaviors is of little use to the novice or preservice teacher if these dispositions cannot be easily taught and acquired, either in a teacher preparation program, or through sustained in-service training. The teacher interview responses provided some insights that address this concern.

Some of the skills or approaches that can be "learned," according to the teachers interviewed, include having a sense of humor, awareness of body language, flexibility with respect to accommodating different learning styles, employing active listening, and developing empathy and patience. Although some of the skills suggested might seem challenging to teach and learn, it was encouraging to discover that highly qualified teachers believe that many of the skills they possess can be successfully conveyed to those with less experience who are willing to work hard to acquire them.

POINTS TO REMEMBER

- *Teachers need to acquire effective behaviors and skills to work successfully with students with disabilities, particularly those with learning and behavioral challenges.*
- *The framework provided by Kennedy (2008) presents three areas of focus in which to cultivate effective teaching skills—namely, (a) personal resources, (b) teacher performance, and (c) teacher effectiveness.*
- *Effective teachers are defined as highly qualified educators who possess a passion for and strong knowledge base in their subject area (Helm, 2007; Mowrer-Reynolds, 2008; Polk, 2006).*
- *Teachers who are effective believe firmly in the potential of all children to learn.*
- *Effective teachers engage in self-reflection and inquiry and demonstrate a "concerned responsiveness" to the learning and social-emotional needs of individual students (Stough and Palmer, 2003, p. 220).*
- *Teacher performance qualities involve practices that occur daily, such as providing optimal learning activities, employing techniques that facilitate student learning, and exploring ways to motivate or entice students to learn (Kennedy, 2008).*
- *Students have expressed, when surveyed, that it is not necessarily the content of the curriculum that peaked their interest in a subject, but rather the quality of the instruction and meaningfulness of the learning activity that influenced their opinions about a teacher and her subject area.*

The primary author can be reached at vance.austin@mville.edu.

REFERENCES

Allen, J., Gregory, A., Mikami, A., Lun, J., Hamre, B., and Pianta, R. (2013). Observations of effective teacher-student interactions in secondary school classrooms: Predicting student achievement with the classroom assessment scoring system-secondary. *School Psychology Review*, 42(1), 76. Retrieved from https://eric.ed.gov/?id=EJ1007218.

Austin, V. L. (2001). Teachers' beliefs about co-teaching. *Remedial and Special Education*, 22(4), 245–55. https://doi.org/10.1177/074193250102200408.

Biddulph, M., and Adey, A. (2004). Pupil perceptions of effective teaching and subject relevance in history and geography at Key Stage 3. *Research in Education*, 71, 18. https://doi.org/10.7227/RIE.71.1.

Billingsley, B. S. (April 2003). *Special education teacher retention and attrition: A critical analysis of the literature. Executive Summary.* Center on Personnel Studies in Special Education (CPSSE) Document No. RS-2E (IDEAS). Retrieved from http://copsse.education.ufl.edu/docs/RS-2E/1/RS-2E.pdf.

Bracey, G. W. (2009). Identify and observe effective teacher behaviors. *Phi Delta Kappan*, 772–73. https://doi.org/10.1177/003172170909001020.

Christophel, D. M. (1990). The relationships among teacher immediacy behaviors, student motivation, and learning. *Communication Education*, 39(4), 323–40. https://doi.org/10.1080/03634529009378813.

Cox, J. (1996). *Your opinion, please!: How to build the best questionnaires in the field of education.* Thousand Oaks, California: Corwin Press.

Crump, C. A. (1996). Teacher immediacy: What students consider to be effective teacher behaviors (ERIC Document No. 390099). Retrieved from http://eric.ed.gov/PDFS/ED390099.pdf.

de Vries, S., Jansen, E. P., Helms-Lorenz, M., and van de Grift, W. J. (2015). Student teachers' participation in learning activities and effective teaching behaviours. *European Journal of Teacher Education,* 38(4), 460–83. https://doi.org/10.1080/02619768.2015.1061990.

Dobud, W. (2016). Exploring adventure therapy as an early intervention for struggling adolescents. *Journal of Outdoor and Environmental Education,* 19(1), 33–41. https://doi.org/ https://eric.ed.gov/?id=EJ1116335.

Goldhaber, D., and Hansen, M. (2017). Race, gender, and teacher testing: How informative a tool is teacher licensure testing? *American Educational Research Journal,* 47(1), 218–51. https://doi.org/10.3102/0002831209348970.

Gourneau, B. (2005). Five attitudes of effective teachers: Implications for teacher training. *Essays in Education,* 13(8). Retrieved from https://www.researchgate.net/publication/251297404_Five_Attitudes_of_Effective_Teachers_Implications_for_Teacher_Training.

Hager, K. D. (2012). Self-monitoring as a strategy to increase student teachers' use of effective teaching practices. *Rural Special Education Quarterly,* 31(4), 9–17. https://doi.org/10.1177/875687051203100403.

Harris, A. (1998). Effective teaching: A review of the literature. *School Leadership and Management,* 18(2), 169–83. https://doi.org/10.1080/13632439869628.

Helm, C. (2007). Teacher dispositions affecting self-esteem and student performance. *Clearing House,* 109–10. https://doi.org/10.3200/TCHS.80.3.109-110.

Helterbran, V. R. (2008). The ideal professor: Student perceptions of effective instructor practices, attitudes, and skills. *Education,* 129(1), 125–38. Retrieved from https://eric.ed.gov/?id=EJ816980.

Hughes, T., and Fredrick, L. (2006). Teaching vocabulary with students with learning disabilities using classwide peer tutoring and constant time delay. *Journal of Behavioral Education,* 15(1), 1–23. https://doi.org/10.1007/s10864-005-9003-5.

Imber, M. (2006). Should teachers be good people? *American School Board Journal,* November, 29–31. Retrieved from http://www.asbj.com/MainMenuCategory/Archive/2006/November.

Jennings, P. A., and Greenberg, M. T. (2009). The prosocial classroom: Teacher social and emotional competence in relation to student and classroom outcomes. *Review of Educational Research,* 79(1), 491–525. https://doi.org/10.3102/0034654308325693.

Kennedy, M. M. (2008). Sorting out teacher quality. *Phi Delta Kappan,* September, 59–63. https://doi.org/10.1177/003172170809000115.

Koutsoulis, M. (2003). *The characteristics of the effective teacher in Cyprus public high school: The students' perspective.* Arlington, VA: American Association of School Administrators. Retrieved from https://eric.ed.gov/?id=ED478761.

Larrivee, B. (2000). Transforming teacher practice: Becoming the critically reflective teacher. *Reflective Practice,* 1(3), 293–307. https://doi.org/10.1080/713693162.

Malow, M. S., and Austin, V. L. (2016). *Mindfulness practices with students classified with EBD: A pilot investigation.* Retrieved from files.eric.ed.gov/fulltext/EJ1103673.pdf.

Mowrer-Reynolds, E. (2008). Pre-service educator perceptions of exemplary teachers. *College Student Journal,* 42(1), 214–24. Retrieved from https://eric.ed.gov/?id=EJ816883.

Nelson, J. R., Maculan, A., Roberts, M. L., and Ohlund, B. J. (2001). Sources of occupational stress for teachers of students with emotional and behavioral disorders. *Journal of Emotional and Behavioral Disorders,* 9(2), 123–30. https://doi.org/10.1177/106342660100900207.

Office of Special Education Programs. (2006). National Center for Education Statistics, Institute of Educational Sciences (IES). *Crime, violence, discipline, and safety in U.S. public schools. Finding from the school survey on crime and safety: 2005–2006.* Retrieved from http://nces.ed.gov/pub search/pusinfo.asp?puid=2007361.

Patton, B., Jolivette, K., and Ramsey, M. (2006). Students with emotional and behavioral disorders can manage their own behavior. *Teaching Exceptional Children,* 39(2), 14–21. https://doi.org/10.1177/004005990603900203.

Polk, J. A. (2006). Traits of effective teachers. *Arts Education Policy Review,* 107(4), 23–29. Retrieved from https://eric.ed.gov/?id=EJ744411.

Pratt, D. (2008). Lina's letters: A 9-year-old's perspective on what matters most in the classroom. *Phi Delta Kappan,* 515–18. Retrieved from Lina's letters: A 9-year-old's perspective on what matters most in the classroom. Retrieved from https://eric.ed.gov/?id=EJ744411.

Rosenfeld, M., and Rosenfeld, S. (2004). Developing teacher sensitivity to individual learning differences. *Educational Psychology,* 24(4), 465–86.

Scanlon, D., and Baker, D. (2012). An accommodations model for the secondary inclusive classroom. *Learning Disability Quarterly,* 35(4), 212–24. https://doi.org/10.1177/0731948712451261.

Scott, T. M., Hirn, R. G., and Alter, P. J. (2014). Teacher instruction as a predictor for student engagement and disruptive behaviors. *Preventing School Failure,* 58(4), 193–200. https://doi.org/10.1080/1045988X.2013.787588.

Scott, T. M., Park, K. L., Swain-Bradway, J., and Landers, E. (2007). Positive behavior support in the classroom: Facilitating behaviorally inclusive learning environments. *International Journal of Behavioral Consultation and Therapy,* 3(2), 223–35. Retrieved from https://eric.ed.gov/?id=EJ801199.

Scruggs, T. E., and Mastropieri, M. A. (2000). The effectiveness of mnemonic instruction for students with learning and behavior problems: An update and research synthesis. *Journal of Behavioral Education,* 10(2/3), 163–73. Retrieved from http://www.jstor.org/stable/41969906.

Singh, K., and Billingsley, B. (1998). Professional support and its effects on teachers' commitment. *Journal of Educational Research,* 91(4), 229–39. https://doi.org/10.1080/00220679809597548.

Stough, L. M., and Palmer, D. J. (2003). Special thinking in special settings: A qualitative study of expert special educators. *Journal of Special Education,* 36(4), 206–22. https://doi.org/10.1177/002246690303600402.

Sutherland, K. S., Lewis-Palmer, T., Stichter, J., and Morgan, P. L. (2008). Examining the influence of teacher behavior and classroom context on the behavioral and academic outcomes for students with emotional or behavioral disorders. *Journal of Special Education,* 41(4), 223–33. https://doi.org/10.1177/0022466907310372.

Topping, K., and Ferguson, N. (2005). Effective literacy teaching behaviors. *Journal of Research in Reading,* 28(2), 125–43. https://doi.org/10.1111/j.1467-9817.2005.00258.x.

van de Grift, W. (2007). Quality of teaching in four European countries: A review of the literature and application of an assessment instrument. *Educational Research,* 49(2), 127–52. Retrieved from https://eric.ed.gov/?id=EJ763428.

Woolfolk, A. (2004). *Educational Psychology.* 9th ed. Boston: Pearson Education.

Chapter Ten

Ready to Learn

Helping Students Develop Positive Learning Outcomes through Effective Classroom Management

Nicholas D. Young and Melissa A. Mumby,
American International College

Teaching the students of the twenty-first century is no easy task. Today's teachers are competing with technology that often distracts or prevents students from learning. Even the most dynamic teachers have difficulties keeping up with the demands of students who are looking for instant gratification (Brackett, 2007). Yet now, more than ever before, teachers are being tasked with increasingly diverse classrooms consisting of a myriad of students with individualized needs. In order to keep up the pace of working with these students and meeting each student's needs, it is crucial that teachers become masters at classroom management (Burden, 2010; Geng, 2011).

The teacher is perhaps the single most important factor affecting student achievement, and the most effective teachers have a multitude of instructional strategies from which they can pull in order to create a learning environment that is beneficial to all students. These teachers are also experts in their content areas and are often skilled in curriculum design. They usually know best when to incorporate certain aspects of the curriculum and when to leave parts out. The most effective teachers are experts in differentiating instruction and, indeed, they know how to manage their classrooms.

What makes a teacher most effective at classroom management, however, is the knowledge that not every discipline issue can be controlled easily (Kottler and Kottler, 2009). There are strategies that can reduce the occurrence of problem behavior, and these teachers understand that it often takes many attempts to reduce negative behavior in the classroom. After all, good classroom managers are made, not born.

EFFECTIVE CLASSROOM MANAGEMENT

Marzano, Marzano, and Pickering (2003) argue that successful teachers understand that there are several aspects of effective classroom management, and teachers should be careful to employ them as they pertain to the group of students in the classroom. A good beginning point is the creation of rules and procedures. Research shows that the implementation of rules has an acute impact on how a child behaves and learns. Keeping rules consistent for all students is key in creating an environment where all students know what is expected (Geng, 2011).

It is also crucial for teachers to properly articulate these rules at the beginning of the year so that there are no gray areas into which students can fall. For example, individual teachers must identify the rules and procedures specific to their own classes. There are schoolwide rules that students must follow, but there are also rules that are explicit to each class. What might be acceptable behavior in math might not be acceptable or safe in a science lab. These rules must be articulated at the beginning and end of class, during transition periods, and during group work, so that students are continually reminded of the expectations (Geng, 2011).

It is also important to include the students in the development of the rules. Creating a discussion around both acceptable and unacceptable behavior allows both the teacher and students to find a common ground (Burden, 2010; Kottler and Kottler, 2009). It also allows the instructor a chance to teach the students about the necessity of rules, and explain that some rules are in place to protect everyone's safety.

A discussion on formal and informal behavior can occur at this time. Some students are unaware that there are socially acceptable ways of behaving in various situations (Kottler and Kottler, 2009). It is the educator's job to make the students aware that there are differences between how they behave and talk at school, as opposed to how they behave and talk while spending time with friends.

Another aspect to effective classroom management suggests that disciplinary interventions are necessary in order to send the message about what will and will not be tolerated. Marzano, Marzano, and Pickering (2003) argue that communication with home can have both positive and negative consequences on student behavior. Oftentimes, a student faces harsh punishment at home for misbehaving at school, and sometimes that comes back to the teacher in the form of worse behavior.

There is also the chance that the parent will not side with the teacher, creating a tense relationship between all parties involved. Parents and students report that positive behavior intervention ranks highest in their opinion of what constitutes effective disciplinary intervention. Instilling fear in a child is the least effective way in getting him or her to want to learn. A student who is afraid of punishment is less likely to put forth effort and will most likely withdraw from the teacher's attempts to reestablish a positive relationship (Burden, 2010).

Fairness in disciplinary intervention is also key to successful classroom management. Marzano, Marzano, and Pickering (2003) suggest that teachers should reinforce positive behavior while providing consequences for negative behavior. However, the rewards are almost certain to outweigh the punishments. Research suggests that students who gain something from their good behavior are more likely to show a consistent pattern of similar behavior than those who are consistently punished for negative behavior (Brackett, 2007; Burden, 2010; Cahill, 2006; Deci and Ryan, 1985; Marzano, Marzano, and Pickering, 2003).

That being said, there must certainly be consequences for students who exhibit behavior that is continually disruptive, inappropriate, or violent. It is important for teachers to give the same consequences to all students who engage in the same behavior to avoid one student from feeling as if the teacher is unfairly singling him or her out for punishment (Burden, 2010). Teachers should record student behavior to ensure that they have a record of rewards and consequences, which can be a way to open up discussion with the student on what is and is not acceptable, and also to gauge the student's understanding of the behavior.

A third aspect of effective classroom management suggests that a solid relationship between students and teachers is critical in gaining student respect. Students who feel cared for are more likely to want to please the teacher. Literature suggests that high dominance in the teacher (strong guidance and clarity of purpose) positively correlates to high cooperation from the student (Burden, 2010; Kottler and Kottler, 2009; Marzano, Marzano, and Pickering, 2003).

Students who respect their teachers are the most likely to follow rules and regulations. While that seems to be an inherent truth of teaching, teachers can oftentimes come across as too overbearing, causing students to turn away or rebel. Teachers should set an appropriate level of dominance in the classroom—that is, encouraging and caring, yet still able to set boundaries between themselves and the students (Kottler and Kottler, 2009; Marzano, Marzano, and Pickering, 2003; Marzano et al., 2005).

Teachers who are dominant use assertive body language and eye contact, yet remain unthreatening to students. They do not raise their voices or become emotional but rather address inappropriate behavior in a calm, nonjudgmental fashion. As Marzano, Marzano, and Pickering (2003) suggest, it is important for teachers to be flexible and fair, assertive and knowledgeable, while remaining aware of the struggles their students are facing both in and out of school. This awareness can help the teacher determine the reason for the negative behavior, while informing his or her choice of consequence.

One final aspect of effective classroom management is a positive mental set. Teachers need to maintain conscious control over their thoughts and reactions in order to best determine an appropriate course of action with a difficult student. Teachers who are attentive to classroom behavior are much more effective at controlling it (Kottler and Kottler, 2009). Keeping emotional objectivity is key in dealing with problem behaviors, especially those that come across as personal to the teacher. If a student knows they have hit a nerve, they are more likely to keep that behavior in their arsenal for future use (Kottler and Kottler, 2009).

Teachers should react immediately but in an objective way that tells the student that he or she is not being judged. It is also helpful for teachers to try to forecast problems before they arise so that they can employ interventions that will prevent a situation from escalating (Marzano et al., 2005). Classroom management, however, is not simply the rules under which the classroom is run. It encompasses much more than that. Rules and regulations cannot be implemented effectively without a strong student-teacher relationship (Burden, 2010; Marzano, Marzano, and Pickering, 2003).

Students who feel as if their opinions matter are much more likely to cooperate with the rules. Teachers who come across as too strict, or even too soft, can negatively impact the way in which students conform to the procedures in a classroom, thus affecting the learning process. Marzano, Marzano, and Pickering (2003) argue that teachers who are appropriately dominant in the classroom are more likely to create students who are comfortable within the boundaries set by the teacher. This dominance also helps to forge that strong bond between the teacher and student, creating a mutually respectful relationship (Kottler and Kottler, 2009).

It is this relationship between student and teacher that may result in increased student motivation and, therefore, better outcomes in teaching and learning (Brackett, 2007). Students who have developed increased trust in their teachers are more easily guided through the education process. Teachers who encourage students to participate in learning for discovery often find that their students are more curious and are better able to self-motivate (McMillan and Hearn, 2008).

Self-motivation and assessment is critical for students to not only become masters of their own learning but also to become contributing members of society (Brackett, 2007; Geng, 2011). Placing the responsibility for behavior and learning on the student is perhaps one of the most effective ways to create a self-sufficient student (Marzano et al., 2005)

SELF-ASSESSMENT AND POSITIVE BEHAVIOR OUTCOMES

No matter the geographical location, there are sure to be students who come to school with both learning and behavioral needs. That being said, these needs are most often seen in urban schools where there is a predominance of students living in poverty, missing at least one parent, suffering from health or emotional impairments, and a plethora of other factors that create difficulties within the classroom (Burden, 2010). Unfortunately, there is not a teacher preparation program that can prepare educators for every situation they will face in the classroom (Brookfield, 2006).

Much of what teachers know about classroom management is derived from their experiences within the classroom, and the trial and error discipline they've used over the years. Many teachers get stuck in the vicious cycle of continually using techniques that have never worked because they just do not know what else to do (Kottler and Kottler, 2009). Susan M. Cahill (2006) argues that children who seem "uncontrollable" are often mislabeled and misunderstood, and by using the same old disciplinary tactics that have not previously worked, the teacher is creating a tense environment for both herself and the student, which may lead to a fixed negative relationship throughout the school year.

Teachers need to take a step back and evaluate what is really troubling about a particular student in order to create an effective plan to change that student's behavior (Kottler and Kottler, 2009). Many teachers report that it is the lack of student motivation that is most troubling. Discussing student motivation "elicits discomfort on the part of instructors for various reasons, the most important being that it has been discussed for eons without clear determination of how to achieve or even define it" (Brackett, 2007, p. 26). It is difficult to measure something that is not tangible, especially when it varies so widely from student to student, and situation to situation. In order to attempt to measure a student's motivation, one must first determine the goals of the particular student.

One must also determine how those goals operate in creating action, thought, and feeling within the student (Maehr, 2001). For example, there are many students who have quite lofty goals yet are not likely to attain them because they are not willing to put forth the effort necessary for achievement. That is not to say that these students are incapable; however, perhaps the goals they aim for do not create the passion necessary for complete dedication. Sadly, many of today's students are unaware of the countless career opportunities available, and they often aspire to the most basic of vocations without any real intrinsic interest.

There is a noted lack of self-connection within our students (McMillan and Hearn, 2008).

In order to become more aware of their own capabilities and, therefore, their own interests, students must become proficient in the self-assessment process (Brackett, 2007; Burden, 2010; University of Nebraska–Lincoln, 2017). This process consists of three parts: self-monitoring, self-judgment, and the implementation of strategies to improve performance (McMillan and Hearn, 2008).

Self-monitoring is necessary in the self-assessment process in that it involves focused attention on a specific aspect of behavior or thinking (University of Nebraska–Lincoln, 2017; Schunk, 2004). Students can begin self-monitoring as early as elementary school and continue the process into college. Research suggests that students who engage in self-monitoring and self-regulation are more likely to remain on task, as well as have an easier time transitioning to new tasks (Brooks and Young, 2011; Cahill, 2006).

Self-monitoring allows students to focus on their own behaviors when performing a task (McMillan and Hearn, 2008). Many of today's students will not work unless there is some sort of reward attached to the preferred outcome. The strategy of self-monitoring allows students to create their own reward system based on what they are able to accomplish without the need for external motivation (Brackett, 2007). Due to the absence of external forces on student motivation, there is an increased level of autonomy automatically given to the student. This creates a feeling of empowerment within the student, causing him or her to feel good about making positive choices (Brooks and Young, 2011).

Another constructive outcome of this strategy is that it prepares students for the levels of independence necessary for college. As students move from high school to postsecondary education, there is the expectation that they will be able to make informed choices, as well as prioritize their work, without a teacher or parent interceding. Students who can perform at this level of independence are generally more successful in the college setting (Brooks and Young, 2011).

Self-judgment, the second step in self-assessment, requires students to evaluate what they know and how much they have to learn (McMillan and Hearn, 2008). In a paper published by Carol Rolheiser and John A. Ross (2013), the authors posit that "students who are taught self-evaluation skills are more likely to persist on difficult tasks, be more confident about their ability, and take greater responsibility for their work" (p. 13). When students have a sense of control, they become self-motivated (Brooks and Young, 2011).

According to self-determination theory, people become motivated by their desire for competence and connectedness (Deci and Ryan, 1985, as cited in Brooks and Young, 2011). This holds especially true for students who have experienced negative attention from teachers due to problem behaviors. Students who are consistently scolded are more likely to continue acting negatively, since they see themselves as unable to perform up to the standards of the teacher, so henceforth, give up trying (Burden, 2010).

The final step in self-assessment suggests that students should implement strategies to improve their performance in the areas in which they have shown a weakness (McMillan and Hearn, 2008). It is necessary for student-teacher interaction at this point, as the teacher provides formative assessment on the student's progress, which in turn, allows students to assess how they are progressing as they are learning, instead of waiting until after instruction has occurred (Brackett, 2007; Brooks and Young, 2011; McMillan and Hearn, 2008).

According to Black and Wiliam (1998), there is "substantial evidence that appropriate formative assessment activities relate positively to student motivation and achievement" (p. 40). When students are given feedback as they perform a task and engage in specific subsequent behaviors, they are able to connect learning and behavior in a meaningful way (Cahill, 2006).

STEPS TO CREATING POSITIVE BEHAVIOR IN THE K–12 CLASSROOM

There is a body of literature available on the ways in which classroom management supports self-assessment as a way to increase positive behavioral outcomes (Brackett, 2007; Brooks and Young, 2011; Burden, 2010; Cahill, 2006; Kottler and Kottler, 2009; Marzano, Marzano, and Pickering, 2003; Marzano, Gaddy, Foseid, Foseid, and Marzano, 2005). Many researchers suggest that educators need to put the onus onto the student as a way of increasing motivation and positive behavior within the classroom.

As Brackett (2007) argues, "the necessity of facts and critical thinking [are] more valuable than simple instructor motivation" (p. 27). That is to say, no matter how optimistic a teacher behaves, he or she cannot be the sole contributing factor in a student's success or failure. Unfortunately, many teachers struggle with this idea in their respective classrooms. Oftentimes, students try to act as passive learners, merely absorbing what is presented as opposed to creating their own learning experiences. It is true that the curriculum demands of the twenty-first century are becoming increasingly more difficult, although not impossible, even for students with learning disabilities.

Many students have trouble believing that they can be successful through their own effort. Brackett (2007) supports this idea by arguing that "goals are closely linked to a varying role of self in determining the nature and direction of action, feelings, and thought" (p. 26). Quite often, students will give up if they do not achieve a specific grade and will often express disgust at their failure to live up to some arbitrary number. It becomes increasingly difficult for educators to guide their students past these feelings of inadequacy that plague them throughout their entire educational careers.

Using the self-assessment model to achieve improved student motivation can be put into practice at all levels of schooling through simple adjustments to everyday practice. Kottler and Kottler (2009) suggest that in order to maintain a learning environment, teachers must work to develop a sense of community within their classrooms. Holding class meetings is one way to encourage students to evaluate their own behavior in the context of how it affects the flow of the whole classroom. Class meetings can help to elicit students' feelings, encouraging them to share their opinions and suggestions; thus, empowering them to become an active part in the learning process (Kottler and Kottler, 2009).

Another way to use self-assessment practices effectively for students of any grade level is to develop a self-reflection questionnaire for students to use either daily or weekly (Marzano et al., 2005).Using these tools for students to assess their own learning and behavior is a way to not only provide useful information for the teacher but also to allow the student to reflect upon an issue after he or she has been removed from the situation. This is especially appropriate for students who have trouble deescalating from conflict. Burden (2010) suggests that teachers encourage particularly volatile students to use self-assessment tools to report on how they've managed their anger.

Kottler and Kottler (2009) argue that it is relationships with students, not the amount of time spent on content, that matter most in teaching. Teachers must rid themselves of the false perception that instruction is the only goal. Students must feel comfortable with their teachers in order to learn in any meaningful way, and if that is to be achieved, teachers must also perform the same types of self-assessments as the students. Reflection is key in delivering more effective instruction and classroom management (Burden, 2010). If we are to require our students to evaluate their own performance, then must we do the same.

Teachers should not be afraid to have students periodically evaluate their instruction methods and delivery to ensure that they are remaining fresh and relevant to the student population (Kottler and Kottler, 2009). In a classroom where reflection and evaluation is the routine, students will become accustomed to looking within themselves to make sense of their learning instead of merely waiting for someone to tell them what to think and how to behave (Brackett, 2007).

FINAL THOUGHTS

Although there are many factors influencing behavior and learning outcomes, teachers can help students become successful in self-regulation by using both effective classroom management strategies and self-assessment methods within the classroom (Brooks and Young, 2011; Burden, 2010; Marzano et al., 2003). Strategies that promote self-monitoring are crucial in placing the responsibility for maintaining acceptable behavior onto the student (Brooks and Young, 2011; Cahill, 2006; Marzano et al., 2003).

It may be true that the school is responsible for teaching students to behave in a responsible manner, but it is the student's responsibility to control his or her own behavior (Marzano et al., 2003). A student who cannot take responsibility for himself or herself in the classroom will be less likely to make positive choices when transitioning into college or the workplace.

As educators who often function as second parents to our students, we must strive to reward good behavior while providing consequences for inappropriate behavior. However, we must also encourage students to evaluate how they make sense of what is or is not acceptable in the classroom.

We must also allow our students to provide a rationale for their behavior at any given time (Burden, 2010). Students who are punished immediately without the opportunity to explain themselves begin to see teachers as dictators who hold all the power in the classroom (Kottler and Kottler, 2009). It is important to remember that teaching is not a power struggle, and sometimes the student is asking for something that he or she doesn't know how to articulate. Encouraging self-monitoring and self-reflection can help both students and teachers develop constructive ways to intersect learning and behavior without creating tension and dissonance.

POINTS TO REMEMBER

- *Effective classroom management includes rules and procedures, behavior management systems, communication with families, disciplinary interventions, and relationship building.*
- *Self-monitoring is a way for students to focus on personal behaviors, creating an intrinsic reward system, which provides autonomy and empowerment.*
- *Self-judgment is the ability of a student to reflect and evaluate both what they do know as well as what they don't in order to increase positive outcomes.*
- *Students must understand their weaknesses and work to overcome them by connecting learning and behavior.*
- *A sense of community reduces unwanted behaviors. This can be accomplished through class meetings, group norms, self-reflections, and evaluations.*

The primary author can be reached at nyoung1191@aol.com.

REFERENCES

Black, P., and Wiliam, D. (1998). Assessment and classroom learning. *Assessment in Education,* 5(1), 7–74. https://doi.org/10.1080/0969595980050102.

Brackett, V. (2007). Inspiring student self-motivation. *Student Motivation.* Vol. 2, 26–31. Retrieved from files.eric.ed.gov/fulltext/EJ864275.pdf.

Brookfield, S. D. (2006). *The skillful teacher.* 2nd ed. San Francisco: Jossey-Bass.

Brooks, C. F., and Young, S. L. (2011). Are choice-making opportunities needed in the classroom? Using self-determination theory to consider student motivation and learner empowerment. *International Journal of Teaching and Learning in Higher Education,* 23(1), 48–59. Retrieved from files.eric.ed.gov/fulltext/EJ938578.pdf.

Burden, P. R. (2010). *Classroom management that works: Creating a successful K–12 learning community.* 4th ed. San Francisco: Wiley.

Cahill, S. M. (2006). Classroom management for kids who won't sit still and other "bad apples." *Teaching Exceptional Children Plus,* 3(1), 1–6. Retrieved from https://eric.ed.gov/?id=EJ967117.

Deci, E. L., and Ryan, R. M. (1985). *Intrinsic motivation and self-determination in human behavior.* New York: Plenum Press.

Geng, G. (2011). Investigation of teachers' verbal and non-verbal strategies for managing attention deficit hyperactivity disorder (ADHD) students' behaviours within a classroom environment. *Australian Journal of Teacher Education,* 36(7), 17–30. Retrieved from https://eric.ed.gov/?id=EJ936995.

Kottler, J. A., and Kottler, E. (2009). *Students who drive you crazy: Succeeding with resistant, unmotivated, and otherwise difficult young people.* 2nd ed. Thousand Oaks, CA: Corwin.

Maehr, M. L. (2001). Goal theory is not dead: Not yet, anyway: A reflection on the special issue. *Education Psychology Review,* 13(2), 177–85. https://doi.org/10.1023/A:1009065404123.

Marzano, R. J., Gaddy, B. B., Foseid, M. C., Foseid, M. P., and Marzano, J. S. (2005). *A handbook for classroom management that works.* Alexandria, VA: Association for Supervision and Curriculum Development.

Marzano, R., Marzano, J., and Pickering, D. J. (2003). *Classroom management that works: Research-based strategies for every teacher.* Alexandria, VA: Association for Supervision and Curriculum Development.

McMillan, J. H., and Hearn, J. (2008). Student self-assessment: The key to stronger student motivation and high achievement. *Educational Horizons,* 40–49. Retrieved from https://eric.ed.gov/?id=EJ815370.

Rolheiser, C., and Ross, J. A. (2013). *Student self-evaluation: What research says and what practice shows.* Retrieved from http://moodle.manistee.org/pluginfile.php/59439/course/section/16807/STUDENT%20SELF-EVALUATION%20WHAT%20RESEARCH%20SAYS%20AND%20WHAT%20PRACTICE%20SHOWS.pdf.

Schunk, D. H. (2004). *Learning theories: An educational perspective.* Upper Saddle River, NJ: Merrill Prentice-Hall.

University of Nebraska–Lincoln. (2017). Self-Regulation. *College of Education and Human Sciences: Special Education and Communication Disorders.* Retrieved from https://cehs.unl.edu/secd/self-regulation/.

About the Primary Authors

Nicholas D. Young, PhD, EdD, has worked in diverse educational roles for more than twenty-eight years, serving as a principal, special education director, graduate professor, graduate program director, graduate dean, and longtime superintendent of schools. He was named the Massachusetts Superintendent of the Year; and he completed a distinguished Fulbright program focused on the Japanese educational system through the collegiate level. Dr. Young is the recipient of numerous other honors and recognitions, including the General Douglas MacArthur Award for distinguished civilian and military leadership and the Vice Admiral John T. Hayward Award for exemplary scholarship. He holds several graduate degrees, including a PhD in educational administration and an EdD in educational psychology.

Dr. Young has served in the US Army and US Army Reserves combined for over thirty-three years; and he graduated with distinction from the US Air War College, the US Army War College, and the US Navy War College. After completing a series of senior leadership assignments in the US Army Reserves as the commanding officer of the 287th Medical Company (DS), the 405th Area Support Company (DS), the 405th Combat Support Hospital, and the 399 Combat Support Hospital, he transitioned to his current military position as a faculty instructor at the US Army War College in Carlisle, Pennsylvania. He currently holds the rank of colonel.

Dr. Young is also a regular presenter at state, national, and international conferences; and he has written many books, book chapters, and/or articles on various topics in education, counseling, and psychology. Some of his most recent books include *Wrestling with Writing: Effective Strategies for Struggling Students* (in press); *Emotions in Education: Promoting Positive Mental Health in Students with Learning Disabilities* (2018); *Floundering to Fluent: Reaching and Teaching the Struggling Student* (in press); *From Lec-*

ture Hall to Laptop: Opportunities, Challenges, and the Continuing Evolution of Virtual Learning in Higher Education (2018); *The Power of the Professoriate: Demands, Challenges, and Opportunities in 21st Century Higher Education* (2017); *To Campus with Confidence: Promoting a Smooth Transition to College for Students with Learning Disabilities* (2017); *Educational Entrepreneurship: Promoting Public-Private Partnerships for the 21st Century* (2015); *Beyond the Bedtime Story: Promoting Reading Development during the Middle School Years* (2015); *Betwixt and Between: Understanding and Meeting the Social and Emotional Developmental Needs of Students During the Middle School Transition Years* (2014); *Learning Style Perspectives: Impact upon the Classroom* (3rd ed., 2014); *Collapsing Educational Boundaries from Preschool to PhD: Building Bridges across the Educational Spectrum* (2013); *Transforming Special Education Practices: A Primer for School Administrators and Policy Makers* (2012); and *Powerful Partners in Student Success: Schools, Families and Communities* (2012). He also coauthored several children's books to include the popular series *I Am Full of Possibilities*. Dr. Young may be contacted directly at nyoung1191@aol.com.

Kristen Bonanno-Sotiropoulos, MS, has worked in education at various levels for more than a dozen years. Her professional career within K–12 public education included roles as a special education teacher and special education administrator at the elementary and middle-school levels. After her tenure in K–12, she transitioned to higher education to teach undergraduate and graduate courses as an assistant professor of special education at Springfield College located in Springfield, Massachusetts. From there, she moved to Bay Path University as an assistant professor and coordinator of the Special Education Graduate Programs. Professor Bonanno-Sotiropoulos received her bachelor of science in liberal studies and elementary education with academic distinction as well as a master of science in moderate disabilities from Bay Path University. She is currently an EdD in educational leadership and supervision candidate at American International College, where she is focusing her research on evidenced-based special education practices. She has coauthored a series of book chapters related to the unique needs of struggling readers as well as how higher education institutions can assist special needs students with making a successful transition to college. Her current research interests include, among other areas, effective instructional programs and practices to assist learning-disabled students with meeting rigorous academic expectations at all academic levels from preschool to college. Professor Bonanno-Sotiropoulos has become a regular presenter at regional and national conferences and can be reached by email at kbsotiropoulos@baypath.edu.

Teresa A. Citro is the chief executive officer of Learning Disabilities Worldwide, Inc. and the founder and president of Thread of Hope, Inc. Ms. Citro is a graduate of Tufts New England Medical School and Northeastern University, Boston. She has coedited several books on a wide range of topics in special education and has coauthored a popular children's series *I Am Full of Possibilities*. Furthermore, Ms. Citro is the coeditor of two peer review journals: *Learning Disabilities: A Contemporary Journal* and *Insights on Learning Disabilities from Prevailing Theories to Validated Practices*. She is the mother of two young children. She resides in Boston, Massachusetts.